Speaking Silence

Speaking Silence: History, Politics and Psychology

(A Book on Proceedings of the UGC Sponsored National Seminar)

Editors
Dr Pratyush Vatsala
&
Dr Sucheta Chaturvedi

Editorial Assistance
Ratnakar, Ojaswini & Avantika

GYAN

ISBN: 978-81-212-2000-2

Published, 2019
Published by

Gyan Publishing House
5, Ansari Road
Daryaganj, New Delhi-110002
Phone: 011-47034999, 9811692060
www.gyanbooks.com
E-mail: books@gyanbooks.com

Printed at: G. Print Process, Delhi.

Contents

Part - III

Silence and the Subaltern Consciousness

Part - IV

Revisiting Silent Self/S: Engagement with Theory and Genre

Part - V
Silence and Resistance; and/as Punishment

Preface

The troubled relationship between silence and resistance provokes an engagement with the burden of silence and the subaltern consciousness there in. On the other hand an exploration of this theme vis-a-vis silence in Women's autobiographies initiates a dialogue with silence and/ as punishment. Another significant dialectic of silence lies embedded in the narratives of the diasporic writers who engage with the cultural dilemmas faced by them. We are compelled to investigate the philosophy of silence and communicate with the existential silence that has been offered by several literatures and cultures. At the same time, silence in the theatre and cinema enchants us with its powerful and ironical potential for discursive engagements with the moving image.

The idea of the seminar on "Speaking Silence: History, Politics and Psychology" was drawn from a student seminar on the theme of silence. We realized that the binaries of speech and silence have intrigued literary critics and scholars alike. The paradoxical nature of silence endows it with the power of communication making it a Janus- faced trope. The opportunity to explore the dynamics of silence through literature, history, politics and psychology has been a fruitful endeavour accompanied by the anxiety that marks such a cerebral engagement. The book of proceeding is the outcome of the exploration of the theme navigating through the sub – themes such as breaking silence in our world; silence and politics ; the philosophy of silence. We pondered over the debate of silence as agency and silence and agency during the seminar. The rich theme offered a spectrum of numerous sub- themes such as ' Breaking Silence in Our World'; 'Silence and Politics,' Silence and Agency', 'Silence as Agency'. Other engagements with the theme resulted in the fruitful exploration of the theme of silence and society, silence and history through the abyss of silence.

The UGC sponsored National Seminar, Speaking Silence: History, Politics and Psychology organized by the English Department of Lakshmibai College held on 23 and 24 October 2019 gave us an opportunity to navigate through the theme of silence in literature and culture. We wish to thank the UGC for supporting us in this interesting journey. We also take this opportunity to thank our colleagues of the department of English who have assisted us in organising this national seminar and the participants who overwhelmed us with their speech and presentations on the theme.

Pratyush Vatsala &
Sucheta Chaturvedi

Acknowledgement

We thank the University Grants Commission for sponsoring this event and providing support for publishing the Proceedings of the National Seminar on Speaking Silence History Politics and Psychology which was held on 23 and 24 October 2019. We thank our esteemed guests for sharing their thoughts on the occasion. We also take this opportunity to thank our paper presenters who made meaningful contribution to the seminar. The Department of English Lakshmibai College deserves applause for organizing this successful academic exercise.

Part - I

Mapping Silence through History, Literature and Cinema

1

Engaging with Wordlessness in Research and with(in) the Researcher

—Anjali Verma

> *"All year, I have felt like one of those oppositional buds (of a flower) that never opens. You know the ones I mean: they have such potential. You can wait forever but they never open."* – **Frances Sommer Anderson (2007)**.

This paper considers the silences one experiences in writing, especially in the context of academics and research. It writes about the contours of what could be stated as a writer's block and explores what lies beyond it.

There are times when one may find themselves full of ideas and thoughts but is unable to articulate it to themselves or to others, and to give it a word-like form. What brings about this silence? What brings about this silence in *me* as a Psychoanalytic Researcher? Further questions could be asked like: what does my body experience when I am unable to articulate my thoughts; what does it get in touch within the clinic and my field? Moreover, as a person belonging to a certain social background in the Indian context doing academic research, what is that which prevents my body from speaking?

This paper tries to look at a peculiar form of Silence in academicians and researchers, who are at a loss of words to express themselves. A silence which creates frustration and suffocation in writer. I have gone through this frustration lately. Frustration of not performing well or not performing at all in my field. I almost alienated myself from the group at College and nobody knew what was happening with me. I also did not know what was happening to me. But I could see this silence silently brewing in me. Lately, I have found this experience meaningful and decided to use it rather giving it permission to doom me. It took me courage to look within and understand my difficulties to unable to perform and to unable to write for my research or for any assessments. It took courage to use the painful feelings, and to sit with them compassionately and ultimately to use it to produce something meaningful out of it. This paper is the product of what I have experienced in last one year and a half.

I am a Dalit woman, and come from a joint family. My grandparents did not get formal education. My parents and their siblings got education but circumstances were such that they could not (and few of them did not) pursue higher studies. Survival and making money was important back then. They have faced discrimination by society as well as by their own relatives who were well educated and were financially stable. My father and his siblings were determined that they will not let their children suffer the way they did. So for them the only mean to not suffer was to educate their children. Education became status symbol in my family. It was given the first priority. They sent their children to Private schools. I noticed pride in my parents' voice when they told everyone that their child has got admission in English medium school. Today when I reflect back to that incident, I not only think they were proud but they were also hopeful. Hopeful that like others, their children will also achieve their dreams. Hopeful that no one would now stop them from growing. It gave hopes to elders in my family to earn tirelessly to upgrade their life and improve social status, and they tried to give best to their children. Anand Mahanand in his paper- *English in deprived contexts- a case of Dalit learners-* writes,

> "The purpose of education is to liberate human beings from ignorance and lead them towards light. It helps us to realise our potential and make the maximum use of them. A Sanskrit quote says: 'Saa Vidya Yaa Vimuktyaye'. It roughly means, 'Education is That Which Liberates'. Education does liberate us from darkness, superstitions, bondages of slavery, and social evils like caste and gender oppression. This is more relevant to the Dalits and the deprived classes."

At home I was constantly surrounded by the stories of how family members and members in my own community faced discrimination at school and/or workplace. I have never faced discrimination in my school or college life but I was scared to reveal my identity to others. I have carried inter-generational trauma in me.

Government supports Dalits and other deprived classes with regard to children's admissions in schools as well as in Colleges. I have doubted myself when I got admission in Under-graduation and Post-graduation program. I have always felt that I have got seat on the basis of quota and not on my efforts or marks. I was in constant guilt. I was afraid to participate in classes. Nobody made me feel inferior but I felt inferior in front of everyone. "Do I deserve to be in this class? I got admission in one of the "classy" subjects, that is- Psychology, do I deserve it? will I understand this subject? Is it meant for me?" And when I got admission in M.Phil. program thoughts like- "How come I came so far? Was it a fluke or I actually worked hard to reach here?" started bothering me. This self-doubt has always kept me two steps backward and I have always doubted my capacity.

My siblings and cousins are mostly Engineers and management students. I am the first generation researcher in my family. As my sister says- "the most educated woman in our family". I am privileged to reach here but I hold guilt as well. My ancestors could not get this opportunity and exposure. Everyone at home has great expectations from me, I too have high hopes for myself that I will contribute something in this World. But with these hopes and expectations also comes fears and pressure to "perform" because I have this (unconscious) belief that I represent my whole community. Why I have put unconscious in brackets one might wonder. Well, I am not sure whether this belief is my own or I am carrying someone else's belief in me. Dalits were marginalised. Their voices have been unheard. Do I have courage to speak? Speak in front of the world? Will "they" listen to "me"? Am I comfortable and feel safe to share this voice with myself and with "them", or should I just keep it to myself as it will be just any other voice.

These self-doubts held me back and I faced a major writer's block. After second semester of M.Phil. program, I could not submit my assignments on time and it started piling up on my shoulders. My participation in class started reducing to the point when I stopped coming for it. This feeling- of not able to perform- paralysed me in the middle of the program, which was quite threatening and deadening.

With the help of my personal analysis I have discovered that I understand better through my body and I create visual images of my experiences, and it gets difficult for me to give words to my sensorial experiences. I resonated with Frances Sommer Anderson's paper- "*At a loss of words and feelings*". She is A New York based Psychoanalyst. She express her difficulty to write a paper for the book- "Bodies in treatment- *the unspoken dimension*". She has beautifully and creatively expressed her writer's block that stayed for one whole year with it, and used it to form a base for her writing. She empowered herself with her own challenges and shares her experience openly with the world. She writes-

> "Despite many years of formal education and evidence of mastery in some areas, I still feel at a loss when I confront dense, highly conceptual verbal and quantitative material. In contrast, when I meet someone for the first time or consult with a new

patient, I "know" a lot immediately, even though I cannot always articulate what I "know" in my body. I rely heavily on sub-symbolic and nonverbal symbolic modes of processing as an analyst and often find it difficult to articulate the complexity of my awareness in discussions with colleagues and when writing. I was afraid I could not convey what I needed to in narrative form. It seems like an overwhelming project, and I discovered that I did not want to work so hard. All year, I have felt like one of those oppositional buds (of a flower) that never opens. You know the ones I mean: they have such potential. You can wait forever but they never open. I felt as if I would never open. But I did. What I wrote during the year was self-conscious and stilted, too studious, dead. What helped me open up was taking in the beauty and wonder of the peonies, staying with the feelings they evoked, and starting to write from that place. I have a highly conflictual relationship with words… I respond readily to color, texture, form, movement, facial expression, and posture and to the pitch, volume, rhythm, inflection, and intonation of spoken language… I was, and still am, in awe of and envy people who seems to be able to articulate concepts and feelings effortlessly, fluidly, eloquently. I experience an unbridgeable gap between my interoceptive, and kinaesthetic experience and what I convey about those aspects of experience in words"

Limited time in hand and demand from the field, puts a researcher into an unsettling position. Body and mind demands time to stay with the idea and meditate on it for a while, which I also like calling it gestation period. One has to stay with pleasant (as few thoughts have developed) and unpleasant (as those thoughts do not necessarily help you reach your goals) feelings in this period. Sometimes, it is difficult to convert bodily, emotional, imagistic and even cognitive elements into definite words and sentences (Frances S. Anderson).

There is a clinical case in which client is not able to perform in her class and has lost faith in her thoughts and expressions.

I would like to bring in a vignette from my clinical work with a young woman.

Sanya (name changed) is 21 year old and is in third semester of Masters program. She is taking therapy sessions from *Ehsaas* clinic of Ambedkar University Delhi. She reported that she gets anxious in front of others and she doesn't like to attend college. It is difficult for her to bring her unique ideas in front of the class. She is not happy with the work she does. She does not feel like writing for her assignments. But once she does, she writes endlessly and expresses her ideas but she feels it is useless as there is no proper structure or definite shape to the thoughts she has expressed. She thinks her thoughts does not collaborate with the readings she refers to. She find other students too bright and knowledgeable. She is in awe how her classmates remembers different theorists. Because she is unable to retrieve information when needed, she starts to doubt her own knowledge, wisdom and creative ideas. She feels less in front of everyone. She always feel inadequate and has started doubting her existence. She does not know what she is doing.

Sanya gets anxious to turn up for group presentations or solo presentation. Her wish is to get absent and till the last moment she has to convince herself to get ready for it. In group discussions, or presentation, she wants to end up presenting as soon as possible. Her body trembles and gets cold feet. She also expresses in sessions how stupid she felt by not giving herself time. She prepares for this event in advance and yet she is unable to perform when time comes. And choose to remain unheard. After exploration, Sanya and I understood that it is not true that she didn't have voice, in fact she felt that her creation is of no use to anyone. It has no meaning. She want to express herself in classes as well as in her writings, but this fear of judgement and grading stops her to take a road to creativity.

What is this relationship of creative writing and academicians? Why one (and I am majorly talking about adults) is not proud to present this creative side or make his creativity a part of his writing?

Is it too difficult or seems challenging to play with thoughts and ideas in assignments, or research paper or dissertation? Why is imagination getting paralysed in formal settings? children are creative and it reflects in their make belief games. They are not ashamed of bringing it in front of others. But are others comfortable in seeing this play? Such plays are raw and are not tinted with sophistication. Children become whatever they would like to and it is meaningful to them. But is it meaningful for an adult? Sigmund Freud in his paper- "*Creative Writers And Day Dreaming*" (1908) writes-

> "should we not look for the first traces of imaginative activity as early as in childhood? The child's best-loved and most intense occupation is with his play or games. Might we not say that every child at play behaves like a creative writer, in that he creates world of his own, or rather, rearranges the things of his world in a new way which pleases him? it would be wrong to think he does not take that world seriously." (Freud 1908)

If a child takes his creative play seriously, then what happens to the same person when he grows up into an adult? Why does he restrict himself to not express himself in the same way as he used to do in the childhood, I ask. Freud writes-

> "...the growing child, when he stops playing, gives up nothing but the link with real objects; instead of *playing,* he now *phantasies.* [...]peoples phantasies are less easy to observe than the play of children. The child, [...] does not conceal it from them (adults). The adult, on the contrary, is ashamed of his phantasies and hides them from other people. [...] On the one hand, he knows that he is expected not to go on playing and phantasying any longer, but to act in the real world; on the other hand, some of the wishes which give rise to phantasies are of a kind which it is essential to conceal. Thus he is ashamed of his phantasies as being childish and as being unpermissible." (Freud 1908)

This silence in adults (researchers) stems from being a part of a world that favours mere (re) production; of materials as well as ideas. One silences the self to be a part of identical perfection, of high yielding words and an alienated self that does not know what to do with itself. A self that purposefully it seems, chooses to not perform, does not write beautiful words and begins to withdraw as its made to feel that its unheard voice is not valuable. This prevail low self esteem and mental health issues that researchers and academicians may develop in such a context.

Conclusion

This writing engages with the question that is it important to open ourselves to Silence in academia, and make or give some meaning to the non-verbal and unarticulated form of thoughts, who have a capacity for expression, if not in words but other forms. How would such "re-stroying", "re-wrtiting" and "re-visiting" look like? Voices that are not just marginalised within the academic world, but also marginalised within. And when one goes to recover this marginalised self, what could one unearth? Would we be able to find another way of speaking, another way of working our lost selves.

Works Cited

Anderson, F. S., ed. (July 2007), *Bodies In Treatment: The Unspoken Dimension.* New York: The Analytic Press

Anderson, F.S. (2007) "At a loss for words and feelings: A psychoanalyst reflects on experiencing bodywork" In *Bodies in Treatment: The Unspoken Dimension.*

Lakshmanan, C (2014) "Understanding The Dalits' Perspective On English Language Education" In *English In The Dalit context.* New Delhi: Orient Blackswan Private Limited

Freud, S. (1995). Creative Writers and Day-dreaming (1908). In Person E., Fonagy P., & Figueira S. (Eds.), *On Freud's "Creative Writers and Day-dreaming"* (pp. 1-14). New Haven; London: Yale University Press. doi:10.2307/j.ctt2250vrw.5

2

The Other Side of Silence: Literature from the North-East

— ***Shibani Phukan***

Even I have words/I can clay-mould them/I have languages and literatures/ forest songs./They crawl back centuries, earthquakes generational... My history is different, defined/by grandmas, rivers, hills,/singing spring birds behind green trees/and seventeen victories...Even I have words./ Languages, literatures/And stories to tell you/ Are you eager to listen, at all? "Me." Aruni Kashyap.

The term north-east India, a directional place name, enters the Indian lexicon in 1971, more as an administrative concept than a local point of view. The north-east of India, home to the seven states - Assam, Arunachal Pradesh, Manipur, Mizoram, Meghalaya, Nagaland, Tripura, along with the latest entrant, Sikkim, stretching from the foothills of the Himalayas to the tip of the Malaysian Peninsula, is a land of lush green hills, home to the mighty Brahmaputra, the magnificent Hornbill, a land marked by cultural and linguistic diversity, riddled by unimaginable violence and untold miseries. As Sanjoy Hazarika observes, it is a "misshapen strip of land, linked to the rest of the country by a narrow corridor just twenty kilometres wide at its slimmest which is referred to as the Chicken's Neck" (Hazarika 159). The north-east is also, arguably, one of the most neglected regions of India.

This is reflected in the policies, or the lack of them, that every government at the centre has practiced with regard to the region as a whole; even as the north-east continues to hold immense geo-political importance owing to its proximity to our neighbouring nations - China, Bhutan, Nepal, Myanmar, Bangladesh and China. The general neglect also finds expression in the lack of awareness that most people of this country exhibit when they talk about the north-east. In fact, in the absence of knowledge about the north-east, multiple and multiplying myths about the north-east, its people, and their issues; have come to populate general discourse about this region. Such discourse often reduces the region to a stereotype, and its people are pigeon-holed into those prevailing stereotypes. However, this cacophony of silence that has muted the north-east, has in recent times seen a phase of unparalleled resistance. The site of this resistance can firmly and unquestioningly be placed in the burgeoning literature emanating from the north-east. Such literature, has to a great extent served the purpose of transporting the "outsider," the "other," the "marginalised," the "chinky," from the heart of darkness to the mainland, from the periphery to the centre. Thus, through its literature, the north-east of India, hitherto silenced, is finally beginning to find a voice of its own, and tell its own story.

This paper proposes to look at a variety of writings from the various parts of the region, primarily focusing on the genre of the novel, novels such as Mamang Dai's *The Black Hill*, Easterine Kire's *Bitter Wormwood*, Temsula Ao's *Aosenla's Story* and Arupa Patangia Kalita's *The Story of Felanee*. An examination of issues arising out of such a perusal would serve to place the people and their issues in a political-historical-cultural context, and facilitate an examination of the stories through a prism of time, space, location, caste/tribe, and gender. This would be a necessary approach to avoid homogenising the complexity and diversity that any study of the north-east must absolutely recognise, acknowledge and respect. It is also important and worthwhile to point out that almost all the works of literature from the north-east being discussed in this paper is in English, and when one observes the growing popularity of literature from the north-east, it is pertinent to point out that one is mostly referring to the literature from the north-east written in English, or those made available through translations in English. The increasing use of English is significant given the fact that almost every state in the north-east is marked by linguistic richness. Arunachal Pradesh has about twenty five major tribes speaking as many languages, Nagaland has fourteen languages and seventeen dialects; and the same is true in varying degrees for the other states. But it is precisely owing to the limited reach of each of the languages, that the use of English has gained currency as a medium of instruction in schools, as the official language of many of the states, and as a dominant language used in the literature from the north-east. This is not surprising as the advent of print capitalism in the north-east can be traced back to the entry of British colonialism in the region, the translation of the Bible, and the consequent modernising impetus that it provided to the languages of the north-east. The possible weakening or sometimes even the prospect of complete erasure of regional languages and dialects, is perhaps the price that literature from the north-east has had to pay for it to be heard and to make a mark.

A primary impulse that registers its presence rather forcefully when one reads most literature from the north-east, is the almost untrammelled urge to tell its history, of its land, and its people. Historian, Hayden White, in his seminal work, *Metahistory: The Historical Imagination in Nineteenth-Century Europe,* studies the methodology of writing history and concludes that historical writing was influenced by literary writing, primarily in its reliance on narrativising to achieve meaning. A very similar impulse, interestingly in a reverse direction, can be seen at work in many literatures from the north-east, whereby, as Kailash C. Baral notices, "In the absence of authentic histories of most communities in north-east, the creative writers have taken it upon themselves to be cultural historians. Their work provides us the resource for writing alternative histories (Baral 8). This tendency, witnessed in a wide range of literature from various parts of the region, is not surprising at all given the historical and political trauma of untold suffering and marginalisation that the region and its people have been subjected to, and the consequent desire to tell its story, to be heard and to be understood, a tendency that therefore unites the literature of the north-east with that of the subaltern. This retelling of history can be traced to events as far back as the pre-colonial times, running through the British encounter, the region's extremely troubled and disputed inclusion into the Indian nation state, and the violent histories of insurgencies/resistance, and the resultant engagement/confrontation between the "state" and the "non-state" actors. One of the most important periods of Indian history is undisputedly the period of the Freedom Movement, the struggle for independence from the British around which revolves histories of protests and revolts recorded from different parts of the country. However the role played by people of the north-east in resisting, sometimes even successfully, the onslaught of British Colonialism, mostly finds no mention in the pages of Indian history because as Tilottama Misra observes, the north-east has never had the privilege of being at the centre of epistemic enunciation of the mainland. Mamang Dai's *The Black Hill* is a work of historical fiction that takes us back to mid-nineteenth century Arunachal Pradesh, to a time when the British were trying to make inroads into the region and its people. At the centre of the story is the disappearance of a French priest and the unfortunate execution of a local innocent, events recorded by history. In this novel, Mamang Dai sets out to achieve and successfully captures the integrity of the Abors and the Mishmees in resisting the tempting overtures made by the British. This is an important instance of interrogating history as the entire Abor tribe was seen as helping the British garrison in Suddya, whereas Dai labours to prove the point that only a few were responsible for this act. During the narrative, Dai also tells the story of how in 1839, all the Khampti clans of Suddya in Assam had plotted to rise against the British, and the Mishmees of Arunachal Pradesh had extended their help to the Khamptis. As a result, the chief of the Khampti tribe had been stripped of his title and dignity by the British. In another novel, *The Legends of Pensam,* partly fable, partly memoir, partly a narration of oral history; Dai reconstructs an encounter with the British in 1911, during which a British officer and a number of sepoys were killed by the Adis in the village of Komsing. What we today call the north-east of India has had a long and troubled history with the "mainland." Easterine Kire's *Bitter Wormwood* spanning from 1937 to 2007, examines the troubled history of Nagaland through the life and times of its protagonist Mose. Through the eyes of Mose, the novel records the struggle of the Naga people to attain sovereignty, and positions the very struggle, often violent in nature, as their response to historical truths, howsoever inconvenient those might be for the Indian state to negotiate. An appendix to the novel clearly states that the Nagas aren't secessionists, or hostile towards India because they did not break an undertaking for union made with the British colonial masters, prior to their departure. This subversive position, contrary to popular and mainstream history of the Nagas, is repeatedly reiterated and endorsed by Kire through a complex portrayal of events in her novel. This questioning of the accepted and prevalent version of history is consistently found in the works of several writers from this region. But these novels from the north-east aren't historical only in a strictly political sense; many of them consciously work towards a retrieval and reclaiming of a historical past. It is a past untainted, uncorrupted by the arrival of modernism, a harking back to a ritualistic traditional past, to a world populated by lais and shamans, a world where myth meets poetry, a world where dreams foretell the future, where the lyricism of prose evoke the tradition of oral storytelling. Many of these novels from the north-east also focus on personal histories whereby not only the individual's struggles, social and otherwise are mapped; but often, in a culture where community is of great importance, the individual and his or her life is portrayed as shaped by the community he or she belongs to. So while Mose in Kire's novel, who loses his father as a toddler, is nurtured by the entire community; in Temsula Ao's novel *Aosenla's Story,* the protagonist is often presented in situations where individual and even filial rights are ultimately repressed in the "best interests" of the clan or the community.

An obvious outcome of this impetus to tell the history of this region is the ensuing preoccupation with violence that one encounters in almost all literature from the north-east. Sanjib Baruah in an essay titled, "Northeast India: Beyond Counterinsurgency and Developmentalism," makes the frightening observation that, " According to a 2006 count, there are as many as 109 armed rebel groups. Manipur State tops the list with forty…Assam is next on the list with thirty-four rebel groups" (Baruah 39). While the demand for political autonomy is the recurrent theme in rebel narratives, their relations with each other are often one of conflict, wherein like in all stories of violence, it is the common, innocent man who is caught in the crossfire and crosscurrents. So while the victim of violence remains the same, the perpetrators can historically be seen as the government at the centre, with the army at it command; and those whose fight commence with the idealism and patriotic impulses, but degrade to common greed for power and money. As Mose, a former member of the Underground laments in Kire's *Bitter Wormwood*:

> The almost daily killings, the young men on the streets calloused by hate and shouting at everyone in sight and the complete collapse of cultural life - it was unbelievable it would come to this.
>
> The war that they'd begun with India more than 60 years ago was just a war. The Nagas had been fighting against the takeover of their ancestral lands by the new nation of India … He had felt so proud to be a soldier back then, a freedom fighter. But now, these killings, this terrorising of their own people - was this what it had come to? (LOC 157)

This centrality of violence and its impact on ordinary lives is also the focus of most of the stories in Temsula Ao's collection *These Hills Called Home*. The stories chiefly revolve around the Naga insurgency and its consequences. "The Curfew Man" sheds light on the impact of violence in ordinary lives with its very opening lines - "The night curfew was still on because these were troubled times for all in the land. Everything had been plunged into a state of hostility between two warring armies; the one overground labelling the other as rebels fighting against the state and the other, operating from their underground hide-outs and calling the Indian army illegal occupiers of sovereign Naga territories" (34). The price for this conflict is the price of two smashed knee caps that Satemba the protagonist of the story pays. The presence of the army in the north-east has been a constant since the time of Independence, and several legislations such as the Unlawful Activities Prevention Act and the Armed Forces (Special Powers) Act (1958), have reposed unlimited powers on the army, powers which have often been abused in the north-east and evoked tremendous outrage and resistance from its people. This anger of the people is persistently communicated through the literature from the north-east. Kire's *Bitter Wormwood*, reflects on this growing public anger at the atrocities being committed on Naga civilians by the Indian army when the protagonist narrates an incident where "Three members of the Naga National Council had been killed and their bodies displayed publicly in town. People were forced to watch as the soldiers stood guard and mocked the dead men" (LOC 685).

At the centre of violence, perpetrated by the army or its own people, lie the traumatised, raped, maimed, mutilated, murdered bodies of women. This is a familiar trope in stories of violence as the body of the woman functions as a site where the contest is played out, it becomes a site of oppression, a site to mark one's territory, establish control, and hegemony. Temsula Ao's "The Last Song" tells the disturbing story of Apenyo, a young choir singer and her mother, raped and murdered by a young army captain and his men to teach a lesson to the villagers for supposedly helping the underground. The senseless, tragic deaths of countless such young lives is further painfully evoked when the story tells us how these women were buried without even a headstone as their deaths were unnatural. Apenyo and her mother thus become representative of the victims who remain unnamed and unknown. Violence in the north-east has often also resulted out of ethnic and communal clashes. Journalist Sanjoy Hazarika writes about his horrific experience of walking through Nellie after the massacre of 1983 and discovering a woman with a neck slashed from side to side by a machete, pleading for a drink of water. This massacre, regarded as a "laboratory for the ethnic rages" (Hazarika 68) that have since then become widespread, finds no mention in the writings from the north-east perhaps because its people still haven't come to terms with the scale and intensity of violence. But the violence spawned by ethnic clashes and militant organisations like the ULFA, and the price paid by ordinary women struggling to simply eke a living is dispassionately depicted in Arupa Patangia Kalita's novel, *The Story of Felanee.* Fleeing from a scene of a monstrous and barbaric attack during the language riots of the 1960s, Felanee describes stumbling upon something soft, only to discover it was a baby "split through the centre in such a way that only half the head, nose, stomach and legs remained" (Kalita 27). However, what sets apart the women characters that we engage with in the literature from the north-east is their mature response to such violence and their fearless resistance to it. Felanee transforms from this timid and traumatised woman and emerges as a survivor who leads a group of women protestors to sit on a dharna in front of a police station, demanding the release of the men detained within. In *Bitter Wormwood*, Mose's wife, Neilhounuo, once a part of the Underground with the nickname "rifle girl," increasingly wishes for lasting peace to return to their land so that they could raise their children in peace. As she poignantly observes:

> Twenty-one years without any respite. Or any lasting solutions. It was a man's war. If it had been left to the women, maybe they would have talked it over and sorted it out long back. After all, it was they who bore the brunt of the deaths of husbands, lovers, brothers and sons. On both sides. But women did not settle wars. It was unheard of.

> The women's lot was to mourn their dead. And the very next day try to find food for their families. (Kire LOC 1132)

But the women did what they could do, which was to provide support for each other, form a sisterhood on the basis of their shared history, and they found unique and peaceful methods of resistance. In 2004, Manorama Devi, a member of the banned People's Liberation Army was allegedly abducted, raped and killed by the army. As a response to this brutality, a dozen elderly Manipuri women stood naked in front of the army's base in Imphal, as a mark of protest, thus propelling this gruesome incident onto a global centre stage. This peaceful response to an incident of unimaginable violence, underscores the intense desire for the return of peace, which is advocated by most writers of this region. Some, like the late Indira Goswami was actively involved with the process of negotiating peace between the ULFA and the central government and worked as an interlocutor. Others like Temsula Ao, commenting on her stories whose genesis lies in violence that Nagaland has been subjected to, writes:

> These stories … are not about 'historical facts'; nor are they about condemnation, justice or justification of the events which raged through the land like a wildfire half a century ago. On the contrary, what the stories are trying to say is that in such conflicts, there are no winners, only victims and the results can be measured only in human terms. (The Hills x)

If it is untold suffering, the constant threat of violence, the indifference of the the political class that unites the north-east; the consequent desire for peace is an even stronger motivating and unifying factor. In this quest for peace, women – common women of the north-east, movements such as Meira Paibi led by the Meitei community, the Naga Mothers Association, and women writers from the north-east - have been torchbearers, resolutely leading the way forward from darkness to light, paving the way to resistance.

Works Cited

Ao, Temsula. *These Hills Called Home.* New Delhi, Zubaan, 2007.

…*Aosenla's Story*. New Delhi: Zubaan, 2017.

Baral, Kailash C. "Articulating Marginality: Emerging Literatures from Northeast India." *Emerging Literatures from Northeast India: The Dynamics of Culture, Society & Identity.* Ed. Margaret Ch Zama. New Delhi. Sage Publications, 2013. Pp. 4-13.

Baruah, Sanjib. "Northeast India: Beyond Counterinsurgency and Developmentalism." *The Peripheral Centre: Voices from India's Northeast.* Ed. Preeti Gill. New Delhi: Zubaan. 2013. Pp 29-56.

Dai, Mamang. *Legends of Pensam.* New Delhi: Penguin India, 2006.

…*The Black Hill.* New Delhi: Aleph Book Company, 2014. Kindle edition.

Hazarika, Sanjoy. "In Times of Conflict the Real Victims are Women." *The Peripheral Centre: Voices from India's Northeast.* Ed. Preeti Gill. New Delhi: Zubaan, 2013. Pp 66-79.

Kalita, Arupa Patangia. *The Story of Felanee.* Translated by Deepika Phukan. New Delhi: Zubaan, 2011.

Kire, Easterine. *Bitter Wormwood.* New Delhi: Zubaan, 2011. Kindle edition.

Misra, Tilottama edited. *The Oxford Anthology of Writings from North-East India.: Poetry and Essays.* New Delhi: Oxford University Press, 2011.

White, Hayden. *Metahistory: The Historical Imagination in Nineteenth-Century Europe.* London: John Hopkins University Press, 2015.

3

Vat Chouboli Ri: Reading Resistance/ Narrative in Silence

— *Gaurav Kumar*

Rajasthani author Vijaydan Detha's rendering of the folktale of Princess Chouboli is narrated by a humorous voice bordering on the nonsensical. Detha's narrator begins by introducing a perfectly patriarchal world in which all is well, and a *Thakur* likes to shoot a hundred and eight arrows through his terrified wife's nose ring every morning. This description is peppered with ironical quips such as "The *Thakurani* could not possibly have known the extent of her good fortune (37)" and "what right could his wife possibly have to object?" (31). For the first two sections of this long short story, during which the niece of *Thakur*'s manager *Seth* confers with the *Thakurani* and enumerates for her the terrible ways in which she would have exacted her revenge on such a husband, we don't meet or hear anything from Chouboli. Towards the end of the second section, the *Seth's* niece, now forcibly married to the *Thakur* because of the insubordination she demonstrated in her declaration about *Thakur Sa*, finally introduces Chouboli. The niece goads her rogue husband to take up princess Chouboli's challenge instead of being smug about performing these silly archery tricks on his wives. Chouboli meets the reader as a rumor and the *Thakur* as a challenge but we still haven't heard from her. This is doubly interesting for the reader who is aware that she is reading a translated text. In the original Rajasthani version written by Detha, the title of the story is "Vat Chouboli ri", i.e. the tale of Chouboli. Since the genitive marker in this case "ri" implies a feminine subject who possesses, this title can be read in at least two possible ways: the story of, or about Princess Chouboli, and the story told/written/performed by princess Chouboli. The second claim seems weak at this point, but we will come back to it later.

As the reader continues with his reading of the story, she gathers from various accounts by other characters that the princess has taken a vow of absolute silence in the face of an army of male suitors who dream of making her speak four times and thereby winning her hand in marriage. Defined almost entirely by this vow, Chouboli offers her silence as a challenge/obstacle to the narrative of male quest for female beauty as its prize and telos. "Seven times twenty Rajas" have taken up and failed at this challenge and are now languishing in a dungeon, grinding fodder for horses. In the third section of the story, our rogue *Thakur* joins their rank stunned by Chouboli's beauty and defeated by her stubborn silence. This paper intends to analyze the dynamics that constitute this silence, subjectivity and resistance, and the political coordinates of the contexts that seem to construct the princess as a subaltern figure, a mute object to be won in a conquest, thereby hoping to recover some semblance of a subaltern consciousness in Rajasthani folklore.

The persistence of the silence that seems to mark Chouboli's character makes it tempting to situate her as a subaltern within the patriarchal discourse that defines her existence in relation to itself but can never grasp or describe its significance completely. Anybody situated within the hegemonic discourse in relation to which the subaltern has been defined, be it the ruling class or the intellectual-critic who wants to understand the subaltern, will always find that he is unable to establish what Gayatri Chakravarty Spivak calls "a line of communication", unable to understand the complex texts that mark the singularity and shadow of the subaltern. Detha describes the *Thakur's* fate in Chouboli's presence: "He had come to make the princess speak, and here he had himself forgotten how to" (43). The project of 'recovering' the subaltern consciousness has always been a contentious one and has been critiqued by many. For Spivak, the term 'subaltern' represents the "sheer heterogeneity of the decolonized space", "the being on the other side of difference" for the historian-intellectual, and, therefore, is precisely that which cannot be represented, illustrating the limits of discourse (A Critique of Postcolonial Reason 310). In her essay "Subaltern Studies: Deconstructing Historiography", she remarks that the idea of a unitary subaltern consciousness, defined by its peculiar essence/aspects, that is deployed by the famous Subaltern Studies group is merely strategic and their "language seems also to be straining to acknowledge that the subaltern's view, will, presence can be no more than a theoretical fiction to entitle the project of reading" (In Other Worlds 204). In fact, all attempts to recover any autonomous, deliberative consciousness can only lead us to a subaltern subject-effect –"an immense discontinuous network of strands that may be termed politics, ideology, economics, history, sexuality, language and so on"- a sovereign and self-originating subject posited to explain "that which seems to operate as a subject" (204). In the wake of Marx, Freud and Foucault, the idea of a self-present consciousness whose desire, interests and speech originate within itself and are completely aligned, coherent and representable is no longer tenable. What the Subaltern Studies group produce, then, are not transparent texts that give us access to the sovereign subaltern subject, but representations of their object, the subaltern "subject-effect", constructed according to their stated goal of writing histories that could constitute a critique of elite historiography. These representations never manage to grasp the subaltern, to "communicate" with it, for subalternity is the heterogeneity of several texts in a context that together serve as the resistant limit, the vanishing point of representation that confronts us as the silence and shadow that Spivak frequently invokes in her works on the subaltern: "when a line of communication is established between a member of subaltern groups and the circuits of citizenship or institutionality, the subaltern has been inserted into the long road to hegemony" (CPCR 310). It seems that the subalternity that has been named Chouboli in this tale cannot be read by a man. Enter the Seth's niece dressed as a man, determined to free her husband by taking up Chouboli's challenge, since she "knew very well that her lord didn't have it in him to make Chouboli speak" (43).

Through the remaining sections of the story, the *Seth's* niece narrates four riddling stories ending in dilemmas of politics and philosophy, but only after securing the encouragement of various objects in Chouboli's room (her bed, necklace, veil, and lamp) as *hunkara*-givers. In her book *Riddles of Belonging: India in Translation & Other Tales of Possession*, Christi A. Merrill tells us that within the context of oral storytelling in Rajasthan, hunkara "involves not only urging the teller on with the oh's and mm's but also repeating the last phrase spoken at a particularly dramatic moment…trying to answer a rhetorical question…and anticipating what the teller is going to say" (69). The craft of storytelling that *Seth's* niece deploys manages to establish this community crucial to oral storytelling, a community that is dynamic and encourages contentious opinions and suggestions, and, more importantly, tricks Chouboli into joining in by blurting out her solutions to the riddle that each story ends in. Chouboli and the *Seth's* niece thus collaborate to create a discourse and a world that sustains stories and desires without a fixed or final ending or goal. The woman-dressed-as-man and the princess who cannot speak to any man seem to have fallen in love.

Detha's text, of course, is very playful about this desire. In Merrill's English translation, it refers to the *Seth's* niece as "the handsome young suitor" and " this woman", as "he" and "she" within the breadth of a few lines, leaving us unsure about the "gender trouble" that has been unleashed (Judith Butler, 2006). It is, as Madhavi Menon has already pointed out in two of her books *Infinite Variety* and *Indifference to Difference,* notoriously uninterested in fixing desire's trajectory along familiar identitarian coordinates. As Butler's book would tell us, such playful parodying of masculinity in the classical quest narrative enables the deconstruction of its solidity and grandeur, rendering the idea of a singular and privileged "original" ineffective; the original/copy binary becomes as comic as its components. The only certainty in the story at this point is the magnitude of the force with which the niece has been smitten and turned into something like a Sufi poet for whom the journey of love is more important than its object: "It would be as wonderful to have her come into your possession as not" (46). Chouboli seems equally struck by desire even while the reader is denied any access to her thoughts or speech and can only see the dance of smile and irritation on her face: "the way he told stories seemed to cast some sort of spell over her" (65).

On their wedding night, the *Seth's* niece reveals her truth to Chouboli, which the princess is only thrilled to hear. She exclaims: "Truly, there's nothing that could give me more satisfaction than to hear that no man could live up to the challenge of the oath that I took" (80). Earlier in the story, the niece had already surmised the grounds for this reaction: "Someone as lovely as this had no choice but to take such an oath. If such beauty were surrendered too easily, it would only diminish its honor...No man was truly man enough to cross that limit. Chouboli was standing up for the honor of all women on this earth" (67). Chouboli's challenge was basically a call for collaborators in constructing a discourse and community of those who cannot be heard within the patriarchal discourse. Its culmination is a clever but vaguely worded arrangement proposed by the niece at the end of the story, according to which, the three women would live together in bliss and retain the *Thakur* to "watch over (them) like a scarecrow" (81). Chouboli and the niece form a desiring couple that imagines a world and conjugality yet-to-arrive, a liminal heterotopia within heteropatriarchy that cannot be fully articulated yet, but which is saturated with strange and new desires ostensibly dangerous to patriarchy. The movement that culminates in this arrangement is best named as desire and one of its conduits is the act of waiting.

For most of her life, Chouboli has waited for the rightful respondent who will meet her challenge head-on, and waiting, as the likes of Marcel Proust and Sufi poets tell us, is the ground on which desire thrives and runs amok. Desire, which, in Simone De Beauvoir's famous formulation, is a movement towards the other, is suicidal in the sense that it dies once it reaches its object. Waiting ensures its survival by keeping the object away, reconfiguring and enhancing it constantly in memory or anticipation. Chouboli's challenge to her suitors, then, functions as the sting in the tail for the tale of heterosexual male conquest that prolongs her waiting and keeps her desires alive and creatively engaged in imagining myriad worlds and possibilities, while the finest men in the world parade themselves in front of her. It is what helps her create her own love story driven by a desire that could only be described unconscious, one that is evidently unwilling to compromise with mediocre endings, rejecting them over and over for a thousand and one nights, and, finally working them out carefully with the *Seth's* niece. This is "Vat Chouboli ri", after all- the tale co-written by Chouboli. Vaat, It is helpful to recall at this point a point made by folklorists such as A.K. Ramanujan and Komal Kothari: within oral storytelling communities it is primarily the woman- the mother, the grandmother, the aunt or the domestic help- who is the carrier and teller of tales. The final ending of Chouboli's tale, as mentioned already, seems deliberately vague about details and open to possible revisions in future to accommodate the various trajectories and loops of unpredictable desire.

Princess Chouboli, the desiring poet-philosopher, waits and reserves her speech for the most engaging political-ethical dilemmas to be included in the story of her desire. The text playfully reminds us: "Chouboli just sat there...*as if* she were mute and deaf" (47, emphasis mine) to remind us that this silence is deliberate, a zero signifier with the signified that can be rendered as: "I shall not speak". As Chouboli's veil and the *Seth's* niece begin to quarrel over the correct solution to the dilemma in the third story, the narrator tells that Chouboli is furious with rage over their silly argumentation: "she was born with a mouth *only* so she could tell the truth" (70 emphasis mine). The truth of Chouboli's desire and being is too disruptive for patriarchal discourse, too disruptive for any available language perhaps, and, therefore, since the language of her male suitors can only sound nonsensical to her, words hiding behind empty words in infinite regression, unable to capture the newness that her being and desire crave, she has effected what George Steiner calls "retreat from the word", a withdrawal from the discourse of heteropatriarchy and into silence (1998). In a funny take on the Bechdel test, Chouboli cannot talk to men but cannot stop herself from reasoning eloquently with the *Seth's* niece. Her masterful speeches at the end of the four stories narrated by the niece are described as a cannonball, as an unwinding spring, as lighting, and as coming out of flames. This alerts us to the fact that the silence of the subaltern is less a function of their capability to articulate and more a result of the sovereign-subject's arrogant belief that the subaltern can be heard/grasped within the comfortable limits of their discourse and thought.

Silence thus requires careful interpretation and committed elaboration, and in the case of the subaltern can only be understood by straining one's thought and discourse in anticipation of the otherness that one can never be equal or adequate to but must nevertheless hope for-- for the sake of both our epistemological and ethical grounding in the world. It requires humble attention directed towards the singularity of the subaltern's situation and context; the alternative, ironically, would be equal to reproducing the silence that one seeks to make sense of. In Chouboli's case, moreover, the reader-critic has to work with another modality of the subaltern's silence: translation as possession.

Let me remark here that most of us will only read Detha's text in translation and let me recall Nietzsche's account of the erasure of the foreignness of Greek antiquity by the Romans during translation: "They did know the delights of the historical sense; what was past and alien was an embarrassment for them;...

indeed, translation was a form of conquest" (67). Detha writes in a language called 'Rajasthani', a language derived largely from Marwari, which is officially considered an inferior dialect of Hindi, the major language of the Indian state. If Detha's Rajasthani were to be purged of this otherness and considered a mere dialect of Hindi, then the space created by his writing in his local *boli*, would ironically appear not as the 'dog's hole' or 'rat's burrow' that Gilles Deleuze and Felix Guattari expect 'minor' authors to dig (1986) but as a gaping crater, largely incomprehensible to Hindi speakers; Chouboli in Rajasthani can only be read as silence and shadow by most of us. Most Hindi translations of Detha's work have thankfully been vigilant enough to retain a substantial amount of foreignizing elements- Rajasthani vocabulary, idioms, narrative conventions and texture-to highlight the affinities and differences between the languages demarcated as Rajasthani, its major language Hindi and globalizing English. These stories invite a comparative inquiry that should consider the complex relations between the translated and "original" texts and languages (which are already complicated pluralities in Detha's case because his stories have been translated first from multiple versions and idioms of oral Rajasthani into written Rajasthani, and, subsequently, into English via Hindi). If we also remember that Rajasthani itself has at least five major dialects and remains open to becoming/transformations along the vectors of diverse caste, region, gender, sexuality et al, we would understand that Detha's writing is an attempt to create a provisional community for a minority language and literature that keeps shifting its shape, story and goals, like desire on the prowl. As Merrill has suggested, translation for Detha's oeuvre is best understood as *Anuvaad* –"telling in turn", rather than the English trans-lation-"carrying across". Literature, Merrill suggests further, in the case of Detha's oeuvre becomes *Sahitya* in its literal sense: literary writing but also combination and harmony. Detha's Chouboli reaches the Hindi/English reader only through multiple oral versions and translations; she speaks in many tongues that can be only be heard by the discerning and loving reader.

By way of conclusion, I reiterate what this analysis of silence has led us to, an analysis which could very well have been humble silence in the face of fleeting subalternity: Chouboli is a silent subaltern only within the hegemonic discourse, be it that of heteropatriarchy or the monolingual nation. We can very well imagine Chouboli and the Seth's niece talking and giggling as Detha's story ends, mouthing Luce Irigaray's words from *This Sex Which is Not One* about the language of the patriarchal Symbolic in which a woman must not exist except as a mirror or a shadow: "their fatherland, family, home, discourse, imprison us in enclosed spaces where we cannot keep on moving, living, as ourselves. Their properties are our exile. Their enclosures, the death of our love. Their words, the gag upon our lips." (212). We can imagine their struggle to keep writing their story, keep inventing tongues to avoid silence, for they hear Irigaray's exhortation ringing: "If we don't invent a language, if we don't find our body's language, it will have too few gestures to accompany our story. We shall tire of the same ones, and leave our desires unexpressed, unrealized" (214).

Works Cited

Butler, Judith. *Gender Trouble*. New York: Routledge, 2006. Print.

Deleuze, Gilles, and Felix Guattari. Kafka: Toward a Minor Literature. Minneapolis: University of Minnesota Press, 1986. Print.

Irigaray, Luce. *This Sex Which is Not One*. Trans. Catherine Porter and Carolyn Burke. New York: Cornell University Press, 1985. Print.

Menon, Madhavi. *Indifference to Difference: On Queer Universalism*. Minneapolis: University of Minnesota Press, 2015. Print.

---. *Infinite Variety: A History of Desire in India*. New Delhi: Speaking Tiger, 2018. Print.

Merrill, Christi A. and Kailash Kabir, trans. *Chouboli and Other Stories vol. 1*. By Vijaydan Detha. New Delhi: Katha, 2010. Print.

---. *Riddles of Belonging: India in Translation and Other Tales of Possession*. New York: Fordham University Press, 2009. Print.

Nietzsche, Friedrich. "Translations". Trans. Walter Kaufmann. *The Translation Studies Reader*. Ed. Lawrence Venuti. New York: Routledge, 2004. 67-68. Print.

Spivak, Gayatri Chakravorty. (1999) *A Critique of Postcolonial Reason: Towards a History of the Vanishing Present.* Cambridge: Harvard University Press, 1999. Print.

---. *In Other Worlds: Essays in Cultural Politics* New York: Methuen, 1987. Print.

4

Silences: History, Memory and Identity A Study of Seamus Heaney's *Death of a Naturalist* (1966), *Door into the Dark* (1969) and *Wintering Out* (1972)

— ***Prajakta Simon***

With Brexit, the economic and political withdrawal of the United Kingdom from the European Union, Irish sovereignty has been put at stake and exposed its people to newer realities of identity politics. With the rollout, the narrow border between the Republic of Ireland and Northern Ireland that served as free movement area for trade has been put into question. The anxiety of the supposed 'hard' physical border post the rollout inevitably conjures up the violent history and memory of the Troubles in 1960s that saw closure only with the peace agreement of the Good Friday Agreement, 1998, with Northern Ireland as part of UK. With Northern Ireland still being unstable, a case of 'unfinished colonialism', the event has resurfaced the divisions between the Unionists and the Republicans, opening up debates regarding Northern Ireland's postcolonial status. Its political and economic dependency along with geographical closeness with Britain has triggered the Northern Irish people's need and struggle for self-identification. Insecurity about identity and explosion of the historical and temporal continuity has made memory so topical. Memory as a phenomenon of the present with its rootedness in 'space', 'gesture', 'objects' challenges history as the institutionalized 'unarguable fact.' The uncertainty of the future has put the people under an obligation to remember. The act of remembering too entails the act of forgetting. The subjective procedure of selective construction of counter narrative while revisiting memory provides it with a quasi formalized system. If this is so, then, memory as history tends to reduce down to the political. Brexit, as a threat to the distortion of normalcy which portends the decline of utopian vision, I argue, engenders an unquestioning right to 'memory' and 'history' as an ethical responsibility. The supposed threat to the 'present' that is aware of the scars of the past and foresees the future redirects our gaze back to the collective memory and history which serve as a tool to reterritorialize the silenced, repressed and unfulfilled claims to Irish identity.

The surface tensions and sectarian divisions that fermented into the three decades of violence and killings in Northern Ireland had their roots in social and cultural conflicts lurking in the ordinary lives before the first bullets were fired in 1969. Seamus Heaney's early poetry is an important area of study that contains the fault lines in the Northern Irish society. In my study, I engage with questions of contestations of history and memory as I examine the changing notions of identity in contemporary postcolonial Ireland by studying closely his earlier works, *Death of a Naturalist* (1966), *Door into the Dark* (1969) and *Wintering Out* (1972).

Identity in postcolonial Ireland is mired in politics of 'omission', 'exclusion', and 'misrepresentation'. The redefinition of identity highlight the epistemological flaw in the postcolonial paradigm and demand crucial understanding of the postcolonial from the lens of Ireland rather than Ireland being viewed from the lens of the postcolonial. This enterprise requires rethinking of the categories of 'irony', 'enculturation', and 'appropriation.' Seamus Heaney who is generally seen as preoccupied with the past attempts to dismantle the fixation to the narratives derived from memory and history by attempting to revise the default accounts that defines what does it mean to be an 'Irish.' Heaney undertakes the project of 'revisionism' deploying 'memory' and 'history' as conduit of mediation to deconstruct the monolithic narrative that authorize Ireland's exclusion from the paradigm of representation. The act of deconstruction entails teasing out of "strains, fractures, aporias, and antinomies that have been attenuated by the narrative sweep."

For Heaney, homogenization of the Irish with Scotts and British forms the first hurdle towards realization of the 'lost native identity.' The retrieval of the 'lost identity' through memory and history evokes the processes of deterritorialization of Irish identity from the labyrinth of the past and subsequent reterritorialization with enactment of representation with difference. Heaney's relationship with the colonizer is well defined within the matrix of deterritorialization followed by reterritorialization.

In the Irish psyche, "the backward look," an act of revivalism, parallel with the Romantic mode of going back to one's origins has been a potent force in shaping identity not only of the self but rather the entire community. From the very start of his poetic career, we see acts of reclamation of the 'authentic', intentionally, exploring the frontiers between the conscious and the subconscious. The way in which Seamus Heaney reclaims the 'landscape' not only in its natural or raw form, but also recreate it as a mental space mediated by language to represent the concrete reality is suggestive of the fact that he can repossess the 'lost' only by way of "rhetoric of compensation." In retracing the temporal history through memory with the purpose of recuperating the timeless vacuum out of which new order would sprout, Seamus Heaney makes what Mercia Eliade would call "the eternal return." James Joyce calls this meditative act of return to be ritualistic, forming a cycle or circular motion, "gravitating toward the 'centers' in order to repeat the profane as well as sacred acts of creation" that are destructive by nature."

Memory is a bond that connects one to the past, it is 'eternal present' and History is a "dead memory," a reconstruction of the 'presence of the past.' In the construction of memory, people are actually focused more on establishing their memory as "authentic." Its authenticity is unreliable as it is rooted in subjective experience of the objective reality. The reality which it purports through the acts of commemoration and monumentalization promises time travel to the past. In doing so, memory contests with history. In reciprocation, history promises retreat to the archival version of the past. Memory reenacts the past events. In a way it scaffolds history but it does not impact the way history pursues the past. It is because of the differential methodological framework that it employs. History works on evidence, archival authenticity while memory works on the conscious life of the subjects. Memory as a subjective narrative has no authority to justify itself and becomes emotionally acceptable. History, on the other hand is discriminatory as it is driven by the hegemonic tendencies of those in power. If both are unreliable then why should they be ever approached? Why do we read history? It is because it is remedy to counteract forgetting. Now the question arises why do humans tend to forget? It is because humans are action-oriented and unconsciously our mind repels the information which is deemed redundant by our conscious self. The relational gap between history and memory calls for what Pierra Nora suggests, as the new notion of history, 'remomaration.' It is a history which is more interested in 'effects' than in causes.

The 'spatial turn' as Hannah Ewence calls it, in the field of historiography and memory studies emphasises the importance of analysis of the textual, visual and oral representations of the past vis-à-vis landscape. According to Susan Sontag, Individual memory is "unreproducible- it dies with each person." Therefore, there is a need to spread individual memory to the collective so that memory in itself becomes history. Thus, collective memory is not a remembering anymore rather a stipulating. It allows for actualization of the past and positing resistance by negating the hegemonic power structures. This in consequence, leads to the formation of a homogenized subculture against the hegemony of those in power.

Seamus Heaney's first collection of poems *Death of a Naturalist* (1966) emerges as a manifestation of combined effects of the spirit of initiation and exploration of the "presence of the past" that arises from anxiety to legitimize the experiences of the 'present.' For him, the present realized as a mnemonic space is a continuum of tension and fear incarcerated into the liminality of reenactment of the past and servitude to the future. The presence, as a constant experience of disappearance of every 'lived moment' presupposes the 'absences' that goes unrecorded in the realm of representation. Thus, Ranjan Ghosh in an article "It Disturbs Me with a Presence" argues "presence is a state of pre narration; it is also implicated in post narration". The experience of the presence has a pre narrative quality. In other words, the action of conscious human subjects has a pre narrative context that does not exclude the awareness of such motivations that dictated our actions or conduct. This is to say that, 'presence' is originally experienced as "disconnected and fragmentary" and not as a fully manifested structure. Thus, 'presence' is a repository of unarticulated pre narrative experiences that evoke a certain return to the past predicated upon the real and the material.

Walter Benjamin says that "the past carries with it a temporal index by which it is referred to redemption." In other words, articulation of the past through strategic selection of particular moment(s) is intimately related to taking hold of memory as it "flashes up at a moment of danger." To simplify, Jeffrey K. Olick, an American Sociologist, suggests that after the decline of utopian visions post war, the nation states returned to the past because the future could no longer legitimize their present. The past served as a vault of possibilities that had potential to liberate the present.

Digging, influenced by Daniel Corkery's *The Hidden Ireland* (1924) the first poem of *Death of a Naturalist* (1966) deals with the personal memory of the ancestors where the anthropological purpose of the poet is quite evident.. The poem starts with the theatricality of the pen symbolically metamorphosed into a gun. It hints at Heaney's complicated inheritance which he wants both to embrace and depart from. He writes:

Between my finger and my thumb
The squat pen rests; snug as a gun.
(line 1-2, Digging, *Death of a Naturalist*).

The anxiety of being uprooted and dislocated from the point of origin propels the poet to delve into the memory of his father and grandfather as a ritualistic commemoration. Taking cue from Jurgen Habermas, every act of communication with the past on the part of the subject is an attempt to make validity claims. From a Habermasian mode of thinking, memory expresses the claim to authenticity while history expresses the claim to the truth. The struggle between the "truth" and the 'authentic' makes memory compete with history to provide an allusion of reality. In the construction of memory, there is a tendency to establish memory as real. Akin to this notion, Seamus Heaney too tries to give an allusion of reality by promising time travel to his ancestral history. He writes, "I felt that I had let down a shaft into real life." He recalls his father digging:

He rooted out tall tops, buried the bright edge deep
To scatter new potatoes that we picked,
Loving their cool hardness in our hands.
(12-14, Digging, *Death of a Naturalist*).

The palpability of potatoes as expressed in "cool hardness in our hands" creates a sense of perception that was experienced in the past and is continued in the present. This nullifies the discontinuity and the continuum of the spatial-temporal index and initiates the poet's quest for self-definition.

For the second collection, *Door into the Dark,* Seamus Heaney had read *The Bog People,* by P.V.Glob, published 1969, the year of the outbreak of the sectarian violence. The book concerned the bog bodies preserved in the east coast of Jutland, since Iron Age, "naked, strangled or with their throats cut.' The archaeological case study of the bog people was crucial for Heaney as he found 'common ground' between the Iron Age Jutland and violent history of Ireland. 'Bog' in Heaney's formulation serves as a potential site for double exploration, a) The marshy land as a physical structure which preserves the history and past within itself, and, b) the landscape as a mnemonic realm preserving memory of the past of the community seen in larger terms as symbolic of nationalist consciousness. Edna Longley comments," if the bog becomes a symbol of national consciousness, it is not in the manner of an insular, self- righteous nationalism. Heaney is mindful of the fact that the lost homeland is less a territorial locality than an ontological locus whose universal dimensions forever elude the boundaries of a particular nation.

The matter of national consciousness and creating national memory has always remained a troublesome project for Irish poets like Seamus Heaney and James Joyce because it implicates the unnatural relationship with England and thwarted desires of United Ireland. The shifting nature of the bog that turns to thick crust each day and moistens every night suggests that bog as a metaphor for Ireland is a place for change to which no distinct signification could be assigned. Heaney writes:

> *...Our unfenced country*
> *Is bog that keeps crusting*
> *Between the sights of the sun.*
>
> (line 6-8, The Bogland, *Door into the Dark.*)

It is in the third collection of poems, *Wintering Out,* published in the year 1972, that, "the experience of authocthony- the feeling of belonging to a place cosmically, beyond family or ancestral solidarity," begins to shape Heaney's poetic consciousness in political terms. 'The Tollund Man', the first bog body to appear in Heaney's oeuvre offers itself as a site for horrific recreation of the sacrificial past.

It was the result of search for "images and symbols adequate to our predicament." Thomas Docherty observes, the poem is an example of 'anamnesis', a recollection of the past, that brings with itself its internal historicity that disrupts the sense of continuity in the present. The poem heightens Heaney's religious intensity with the deployment of mythic rituals. The invocation to Nerthus, the goddess that demanded sacrificial bridegroom to bed her every fall in promise of rich harvest, had great potential to stir the emotions of the young Irish devotees. This image stirred Heaney to immediately draw parallels with the contemporary sectarian killing in Ireland of 1970s.

In 'The Tollund Man' Heaney empathises deeply with his subject. This empathy deepens as he declares his intention to visit Aarhus, Danish town at the east coast of Jutland, to pay homage to the bog body. The makes the mood of the poem as futural, oriented towards the future. He writes:

> Some day I will go to Aarhus
> To see his peat – brown head,
> The mild pods of his eyelids,
> His pointed skin cap,
> His last gruel of winter seeds
> Caked in his stomach,
> Naked except for
> The cap, noose and girdle, (WO)

Heaney juxtaposes the civilized ritual sacrifice of the Tollund man "which could at least claim the dignity of a religious purpose"...with the atrocity of the 1920s that wiped out the entire generation of a family. Heaney is reminded of the four Catholic brothers who were mutilated and put to death by the Protestant Paramilitary troops. The Tollund Man,' is retreat to the violent history of the past. In doing so, the poet repeats the Irish history to orient the present towards the future. 'The impression of repetition in Irish history is less an indicator of actual historical pattern than of the dominance of a preferred narrative in which the future continuously holds the promise of newness… a future departure from the pattern will finally allow Ireland to 'come to its own.'

In conclusion, one sees that in creating a counter-memory and history, Seamus Heaney is contesting with the other collective schema to pave the way for exploring the transmission and diffusion, and ultimately meaning of this act of representation through revisionism.

Works Cited

Allen, Michael (ed.) *New Casebooks: Seamus Heaney*, New York: St. Martin's Press, 1997. Print.

Assmann, Aleida. "Transformations between History and Memory", in *Social Research: An International Quarterly*, Vol 75, No. 1. Spring, 2008, pp.49-72. Project Muse. Web. Accesssed: 21-07-2017.

Auge, Andrew J. "A Bouyant Migrant line: Seamus Heaney's Deterritorialized Poetics" in *Literature Interpretation Theory*, Taylor and Francis Inc, 2003

Confino, Alon. "Collective Memory and Cultural History: Problems of Method." *American Historical Review,* 102, December 1997: pp. 1386-1403. JSTOR. Web. Accessed. 17-07- 2017

Flannery, Eoin. *Ireland and Postcolonial Studies: Theory, Discourse, Utopia.* UK: Palgrave Macmillan, 2009. Print.

Hart, Henry. *Seamus Heaney: Poet of Contrary Progressions*, Syracuse University Press, 1993.

Heaney, Seamus. *Death of a Naturalist*, Faber and Faber, 1966..

Heaney, Seamus. *Door into the Dark*, Faber and Faber, 1969.

Heaney, Seamus. *Wintering Out*, Faber and Faber, 1972.

Heaney, Seamus. *Preoccupations: Selected Prose,* 1968-1978. Farrar, Straus and Giroux, 1981. Print.

Kiberd, Declan. *Inventing Ireland: The Literature of the Modern Nation*. London: Jonathan Cape, 1995. Print.

O'Brien, Eugene. *Seamus Heaney: Creating Irelands of the Mind*, Dublin: Liffey Press, 2002.

O'Brien, Eugene. *Seamus Heaney and the Place of Writing,* University Press of Florida, 2002. Print.

O'Brien, Eugene. *Seamus Heaney: Searches for Answers* ,London:Pluto, 2003.

Parker, Michael. *Seamus Heaney: The Making of the Poet.*Springers, 12 Oct, 1994.

Tobin, Daniel. *Passage to the Center: Imagination and the Sacred in the Poetry of Seamus Heaney.* Lexington: University Press of Kentucky, 2015.

Part - II

Discursive Engagements with Silence and the Moving Image

1

Untangling 'Her' Silences: Women in Select Hindi Films of Twenty First Century

— *Mercy Jill Jill*

Far from understanding Silence as a negative force, silence must be first understood as an energy that stems from immense mental stability and power. Secondly, it should be understood as a phenomenon that prevails before a revolution that will have its reverberations and ramifications in the realizations of the anticipated subversions. Silence as a force can be read in most discourses of oppression and suppression. In literature and Cinema, various shades of silence can be traced in tangled forms. The paper aims at locating, re-storying, and re-screening the silence of female characters in select Hindi Cinema of twenty first century. Throughout the history and performance of Hindi Cinema, surplus of female characters can be watched as silent on varied pretexts.

However, the paper reads select Hindi films, namely, *Devdas* (2002), *Parineeta* (2005), *Queen* (2013), and *Parched* (2015) in the light of silences the female characters experienced in the contrasting loud circumstances of family ties, patriarchy, caste or the 'force' as it can exist before the culmination of an expected liberation.

Silence, however becomes a path of suffering that may or may not lead to the helm of comfort and power. To be voiceless becomes unmanageable when the sounds inside the self becomes loud. Reading these cinematic narratives, it is understood that the silent women always scream inside and has already begun the revolution with the self. To regain the 'lost voice', the character of Paro in *Devdas* had to listen to the screams inside her own self first. *In Parineeta*, silence in its most powerful form could create vibrations required in a magnitude vaster than the loudness outside. Similarly, the realisation of the strength of a female self, silences Rani in *Queen*, only to assert and impose the desirable consequences of her silence to the end of the film. *Parched*, also voices such deafening cannon shots in a brilliant demeanour.

Silence can be interpreted in multifarious ways. It has different meanings in different circumstances. But silence is always an extended discourse. Silence is a story which is hidden beneath those loud lines of words and noises. when reading, silence is brooded upon and is reeled upon as a lengthy interpolation. Like Bacon said "silence is fermentation of thoughts".

When listening, silence thunders as questions. On watching silence makes a new story, it needs a re-storying and a re- screening. Cinema as a visual medium opens a Pandora's Box gives silence a voice. Sometimes silence is voluntary and sometimes it is involuntary, sometimes it is inevitable, sometimes it needs to be broken. The semantic, connotative, explanational or exegetic meanings of silence are many. Western humanist discourses represent speech as a human agency, and the phraseology of silence then becomes a rupture, a breakage, a fissure, resentment, a crack, a tear, and discontinuity. In this essay Silence is taken have two aspects. Firstly silence as Omission and submission, second, silence as reprisal and defiance. Cinema has various instances of marginal silences. The magnitude of silence that Gender algorithms brings in stands the most significant among other silences in the visual rhetoric. In her book *English Gentlewoman* (1631), Richard Brathwait describes feminine silence— "Silence in a Woman is a moving Rhetoric, winning most, when in words it wooeth least". The dictum talks about the notion of power that silence offers. Silence stands as a substantial discourse in itself. But why are women silent? In the early modern culture loud women were looked down upon. Women were hardly described as an independent being, if in speaking she enters the male discourses, she was sure to be labelled a whore. Here silence appears to be promising approach to early modern women. Then how can silence substitute a surrogate for male dominated discourses? This the essay deciphers using prospective Hindi films used for the study.

'He' was the 'norm' and 'she' was an 'anomaly' to the manifestation. Woman does not have an identity other than being the binary opposite of man. There have always been stereotypes or role models for how a woman should 'perform' the act of being a woman, backed up by the established notions of culture and civilization. Indian Cinema has never endingly reflected this trend of Indian society. The cinema has also unfailingly recorded the progress of women and their rights that twenty-first century Indian society is undergoing. Female characters are sometimes muted throughout the film. The film *Aakrosh* released in 2010 directed by Priyadarshan stands as a precedent for further discussions. The character of Geeta portrayed by Bipasha Basu remains voiceless for the span of almost entire film. the character of Geeta's silence is a discourse of fear. Fear here becomes a factor that can devoice the female character. The film also has poor population consisting of male and female voiceless. The mass is perturbed by another great political power. The study shows how power can mute you down to a great extent. Voice, therefore is as much a sign of lack of the possession of power and agency. It may be that those with the most power and agency are those who are likely to need to speak in the public domain to retain their position. The team of local police in the film is shown as extremely powerful and always have their things done. The female character is physically abused and insulted. Even after all the atrocities committed against her, she is not ready to run away from her husband- the ruthless police inspector. Here again power plays a double game. Geeta is meek in front of the hegemonic patriarchy. But Geeta is not a docile woman for Roshni, the daughter of village head or the diffident villagers. Geeta's silence is in two levels. She is fearful for her own self and her former love Pratap. And Geeta is helpless about the villagers. These are the two manifestations of negative silence that we see in the film Aakrosh. We also, see how silence is broken into another form of silence towards the end of the film. Geeta regains courage and helps the investigating officers against her corrupt husband. This is a serene silence she gets into aware of the fact that she will have to pay for being a voice. This is a silence that can be read like that of the film *Devdas* released in 2002 based on Sarat Chandra Chattopadhyay's novel *Debdas*. The character of Parvathi is a victim of social constraints. Communal impediments can be a hindrance to voice. Parvathi who is initially clattery is abruptly silenced by the power of society to which she submits herself. This societal circle includes her own parents. One decision of Parvathi could have re-storied the plot of *Devdas* which we see does not happen. The articulation between silence and powerlessness is reified across cultures. Its equation presumes a political imperative for an individual or a group who is silenced to gain power, they must activate voice to resist and transform the conditions of their oppression (Malhotra et al. 1) as in the case of villagers in Aakrosh. Visualizing *Devdas* as a performance, it is seen that it is not always patriarchy that is directly hampering female voice, but a social construct. The hero in the film also suffers voicelessness. It is interesting to note how Chattopadhyay silences a western educated hero when planted in the Indian cultural stratum were patriarchy is the norm and voice is a legacy inherited by the powerful among them. If Paro had waited for Devdas to come back before her marriage to the Takur, the story would have had a different turn. Paru and Devdas reconciles on the day of Parvathi's marriage. But unfortunately, Parvathi is engulfed in the spell of profound silence. She is overlaid by the limitation of her familial and communal culpability. She is further silent at her husband's house when her husband declares his love for his former wife. These silences are ruptured at the end of the film. But combined enormity of the silence remains the same. Another instance of such quietude is seen in the film *Parched* directed by Leena Yadav in 2015. Silence in Parched is illustrated in a different way. Silence here acts in the apparel of resistance. Mild linguistic resistance. The character of Lajjo, played by Radhika Apte abused by her husband Manoj. She is silent here, but is not completely silent. She is partially gagged out of fear of her husband but manage to share her difficulties to her companion Rani. In the vent of silence between her abuse from the husband and her own loud self, Lajjo goes in the dream to achieve she always wanted-to get impregnated. Lajjo on the first place would have had a completely different discourse if she was not silent. She could have told her husband about his infertility. Three women shown in the film have numerous moments of silence. But the character who is spell bound silent is the character of child bride Janaki. This character is silent throughout the film except for a liberation trip with three other women in question. Revisiting Janaki's character, she is not given any kind of voice even after being more educated than the other characters who control her life. Janaki loves books, Janaki is in love with her childhood friend. She is not ready to marry. She does not like Gulabo her husband. She cuts her hair off as a sign of silent resistance. In the introduction to *Listening to Silences: New Essays in Feminist Criticism,* Elaine Hedges quotes, Frederic Jameson's words on texts, "they are "not as seamless webs and triumphant narrative progressions" but as works with Gaps and breaks, discontinuities and absences-focused on silences that were intrinsic rather than external to the text. Such silences in turn, might reveal reticences culturally imposed upon women, the working of repressed ideology, or, alternatively, women's deployment of silence as a form of resistance to the dominant discourse. These gaps and breaks are sometimes highly cryptic. For instance, the film *Parineeta,* which was released in 2005 has a peculiar silence, partially bilateral and occasionally unilateral. The film stems from the silence of female and male lead. The female protagonist Lolita is here silenced by the male hero Shekar. She tries to initiate conversations which are all disregarded by the male character. If the silence of the character is re-screened then Lolita, the female lead will have volumes to speak of hero's father, how she and her family was hedged in by him and how he tried to seize their property, how he insulted her as a female. She would also talk about how Girish, a family acquaintance from London proposed her for marriage and how she refused him saying she was already married and how much she loves her husband Shekar. But this discourse is missing from Lolita in the film. instead these gaps are replenished by Girish's conversation with Shekar on the day of his second marriage. But why was the silence of Lolita so powerful that she even let her husband do whatever he likes irrespective of her wishes. "Silence is paradoxical. It is paradoxical because it is absence of speech and therefore of meaning or communicative power, but also, like speech, matter of interpretation. "Silence is a present absence" says Parpart in the forward to her book *Rethinking Silence, Voice and Agency in Contested Gendered Terrains: Beyond*. Silence is very much present as absence of voice, and this absence is so powerful that a agency had to intervene to break and re-discourse the voicelessness. In a communicative situation it matters whether or not we choose to talk. The possibility of speech renders its absence potentially meaningful. Bergmann asks, "how can this nothing that we call silence become meaningful for those participating in the conversation?" he answers the question by talking about the contexts that make silence meaningful for the ones taking part in the interactions. Jaworski, another critic says silence can also be when there is nothing relevant to say. This instance can be delineated through the film Queen released in 2014, starring Kangana Ranaut directed by Vikas Behl. The female lead Rani shuns herself after her marriage was cancelled from the fiancé's side. Silence can be all pervasive or targeted. Here the silence was targeted. Rani's initial silence was result of her helplessness and vulnerability. Later silence becomes her choice which she targets towards her fiancé who wants a reconciliation. "Silence can also be regarded because of a gap in time required for cognitive processing...". (Nakane 136) Rani takes sometime to figure out what should be made out of her silence. The uncertainties are very much evident from the reaction and expressions she has whenever there is an encounter of with her target. The film also allows us to re-story her situational silence which happens for the span of twenty-four hours after she was abandoned by her fiancé. This sort of a silence is most expected silences despite the discomfort it causes others, here Rani's parents.

Works Cited

Glenn, Cheryl. *Unspoken: A Rhetoric of Silence.* South Illinois University Press, 1985. Print.

Hedges, Elaine (ed). *Listening to Silences: New Essays in Feminist Criticism.* Oxford University Press, 1994. Print.

Luckyj, Christina. *'A Moving Rhetoricke': Gender and Silence in Early Modern England.* Manchester: Manchester University Press, 2002. Print.

Malhotra, Sheena and Aimee Carrillo (ed) Rowe. *Silence, Feminism, Power: Reflections at the Edges of Sound.* Palgrave Macmillan, 2013. Print.

Nakane, Ikuko. *Silence in Intercultural Communication: Perceptions and performance.* John Benjamin Publishing Company, 2007. Print.

Parpart, Jane L. and Swati (ed) Parashar. *Rethinking Silence, Voice and Agency in Contested Gendered Terrains.* Routledge, 2018. Print.

2

Disability and Visuality: Video Blogs as 'Countervisuality'

—*Jyoti Singh*

This paper brings together two important areas of study, disability studies and visual culture studies. It is an attempt to provide an outline of the presence of disability and its various expressions both in historical and modern day visual culture while using disability studies framework to guide my analysis of video blogs consisting of two YouTube channels, 'Anya Darlow' and 'Squirmy & Grubs'. Similar to recent disability documentary cinema, video blogs represent a "site of resistance and political revision" by focusing on the voices and perspectives of disabled people (Snyder and Mitchell 193). This research paper will also explore theoretical connections between visuality and disability to understand how video blogging holds the space to challenge the existing negative constructs generally associated with physical disability throughout dominant visual culture.

Due to the limited amount of research that explores theoretical links between visual culture studies and disability studies perspective, J. Davis and Marquard Smith were prompted to initiate the conversation in the *Journal of Visual Culture* regarding the convergence between 'disability' and 'visuality' and how it seeks to explore the ways in which disability and visuality so often constitute one another (132). The authors state that this convergence allows disability to challenge our present conceptions of visuality and encourage us to think of new ways of approaching the problems of the visual (132). For this reason, the common attribute between the two fields of study is the analysis of material adverse effects of representation and a concern for authority. Marquand Smith highlights the importance of observing this convergence by arguing that the theme's issue is their way of forcing the field of visual culture studies to draw its attention to the fact that 'disability' is a structuring and founding principle within one's thinking about visuality.

Disability Studies Scholar, Rosemarie Garland Thomson's work has argued for the understanding of disability studies as part of a larger critical methodology that excavates the meanings of embodied differences and explores how the body has been understood over time (2). She maintains that one of the objectives of disability studies is to transform disability within the dominant cultural imagination, "it conceptualises disability as a representational system rather than a medical problem, a discursive construction rather than a personal misfortune or a bodily flaw" (Thomson 1). She uses this perspective to argue that the body that is perceived as disabled develops into a cultural artefact produced by material, discursive, and aesthetic practices that interpret bodily variation (Thomson 2).

In *The Right to Look*, Nicholas Mirzoeff states that countervisualities are capable of confronting authority's narrow construction of reality by re-imagining and subsequently establishing its alternative (289). According to him, visuality needs to be examined as constitutive of the authority to generate meanings and assert a dominant discourse in which countervisuality is capable of continuously disturb and prevent the materialisation of visuality (289). Taking into account several points raised by Mirzoeff, I will emphasise certain subversive aspects of Video blogs so as to address the question of whether video blogging is a form of countervisuality that is capable of challenging the jurisdiction of dominant forms of visuality. The elaborate analysis of selected YouTube channels will show how video blogging like new documentary cinema, efficiently challenges long-established ways of seeing disability. The analysis will also show how video blogging works as a subversive form of visuality which threatens the dominant and conventional representations of disability in contemporary culture that are too often objectifying and marginalising. In his review of *The Right to look*, Jan Baetens stresses this subversion of countervisuality by arguing that it is not only a way of seeing or an alternative way of looking at the images but also the means to subvert the self authorising tendencies of the hegemonic structures(95). He continues, "it is the attempt to reconfigure visuality as a whole (p. 24) and thus the right to look, which goes even further than just the right to look back, although looking back is the first step towards countervisuality" (95).

Before we begin the analysis, it is crucial to deliberate over the history of visual representations of physical disability as it plays a huge role in determining the current dominant conceptions of physical disability. In her seminal paper, "Integrating Disability, Transforming Feminist Theory", Thomson gathers an array of theoretical formulations and historical materials to emphasise and critically challenge social practices and dominant ideologies of all historical periods that concedes exclusionary attitudes and legitimises discriminatory practices towards disability. She substantiates this contention by demonstrating the premise that anybody with an unusual embodiment is considered to be inferior, or incomplete by presenting the example of Saartie Bartmann. The display of Saartie Bartmann was used to present an image that was grotesque, abnormal and therefore, something worth displaying; it reinforces Thomson's critique of meaningless stigmatisation and stereotyping anything that does not confirm to the ideals of Western thought (7).

In his foundational text, *The Creatures Time Forgot: Photography and Disability Imagery* (1992), David Hevey examines the negative visual representation inherent in the disability photography. Hevey goes on to argue that close examination of photographic representation within an ableist society reveals the oppressive disability imagery, its use as symbols of otherness and how visual consumption of disability is mostly related to the oppression of disabled people (Fraser 40). In *The Enfreakment of Photography*, David Hevey contends with numerous examples that disabled people have been frequently represented but exclusively as figures of otherness (445). Tobin Siebers writing in the same vein declares that disability has been present throughout the history of modern art even though it is not usually recognised as such (Fraser 43). It is important to note that these historical representations of disability were mostly used to rationalise normative standards of non-disabled people which in turn leads to an oppressive understandings of disability.

In addition to the above mentioned studies, disability scholars Don Hevey and Jenny Morris identify ten pervasive stereotypes in the mass media. Most of these are identified to be negative by Colin Barnes (3). These stereotypes include presenting the disabled character "as pitiable and pathetic, as an object of violence, as sinister and evil, as atmosphere or curio, as super cripple, as an object of ridicule, as their own worse and only enemy, as burden, as sexually abnormal, as incapable of participating fully in community life and as normal (it is one-dimensional and does little to reflect the experience of disability)" (Barnes 1992). Thus, most scholars seem to agree that disability has been extensively represented in mainstream culture and used as a cultural commodity for many years. As disabled people have been rarely given a chance to voice or control their own portrayal, their representation has operated at the expense of being portrayed negatively.

The new sources of visuality, new documentary cinema and video blogging have much in common in allowing the disabled to be in charge of his or her representation. According to Mirzoeff, these sources of countervisuality are a way to create forms of change (289). The medium of video blogs and new documentary cinema gives disabled people an opportunity to use their own voice to present their personal experiences and discuss their life of their own accord. It gives them an established platform, where they can represent themselves and their identity in their own way while resisting oppressive representations and changing the way disability is understood as it is used to "create new self- images, new ways to see and be seen, and new ways to see the world" (Mirzoeff 279).

As Internet contributes to the ever growing amount of visual information, it provides a platform for disabled people to advocate for visibility. Similarly, video blogs illustrate a new form of communication and visuality "that doesn't refute impairment"(Snyder & Mitchell 193). Mirzoeff's focus on resistance is clear in his work when he states violent effects of visual authority as practiced on the bodies of the marginalised and how these enactment of visual authority was met with several counteracts and alternative ways of seeing. Similarly, when experiences of disabled people are highly influenced by representations and cultural assumptions about disability, social media is a major source of providing an alternative way of seeing. Therefore, it allows disabled people with video blogs to reach out to as many people as they can to have discussions about inclusion in ways that cultivates fruitful dialogue between both sides. Anya Darlow admits that she would not have been able to spread awareness about her disability and life had it not been for social media platforms like Instagram and YouTube. As a result, social media is being utilised by activists of all kind to connect with other people and create more opportunities for expanding conversations on inclusion and access for all disabled people. Similarly, several disability activists like Anya Darlow and Shane are constantly challenging the notions about disability that society gathers from films that focus on disabled characters. These false conceptions keep people from realising the extent of oppression faced by disabled people in terms of their fighting for access and accommodations.

Video blogger, Anya Darlow is a young paraplegic woman in a wheelchair. She uses her YouTube channel to video blog about her personal journey of living with Spinal cord injury and document the reality of being a disabled young woman in today's society. She is committed to using her channel to tackle stigmas around disability and to help other physically disabled people. She aims to educate and dispel misconceptions around disability in a fun and engaging way by discussing a range of topics, including student life, dating, sexuality, sexual health, physical therapy and other similar issues. This can be seen as extremely revolutionary especially when sexuality and disability continue to remain a taboo topic for disabled people. Her talks on sexuality necessitates her audience to reconsider their preconceived notions around disability by questioning the narrow formulation and cultural stereotypes to which disabled women and their sexuality are generally consigned. In one of her videos, Darlow recalls her difficult experiences of visual objectification that come with negotiating the world when she talks about the ignorance she has to put up with from random strangers when they ignorantly ask, "how did that happen? or why are you like that?", implying that disabled people are obligated to give them an explanation about their medical background. Darlow describes various instances where her wheelchair caused others to stare at her, pity her or just completely reject her suggesting unawareness, misconception and outright hostility from members of the society can combine with inaccessible infrastructure to stop disabled people from living as should be their right. This has not kept Darlow from regularly addressing questions that strangers may have about her experience as a disabled woman and show others that disabled people are wholly capable of leading a satisfying life.

The second YouTube channel that needs to be discussed is run by an interbaled couple, Hannah Alyward and Shane Burcaw, who share their story to erase interbaled couple stigma. Shane was born with Spinal muscular atrophy that causes his muscles to waste away as he grows older. Their video blogs showcase several aspects of their relationship by documenting their day to day lives to help normalise interabled relationships. Their goal is to help other people who may be in a similar relationship and advocate for the disabled community. The difficulty of access and being scrutinised by multiple strangers is highlighted by Hannah when she adds, "The most frustrating thing we have to deal with is the reactions to Shane and our relationship that other people have"(Hannah). They elaborate this further by adding that when they are in public, people are quick to assume that "Shane is Hannah's son, or Hannah is a babysitter or a nurse and Shane is incapable of contributing to their relationship which can be extremely humiliating" (Hannah) and it goes to show how it can cause many disabled people to miss out on a social life. Hence, we can see that disabled people still routinely encounter negative reactions from other members of the public, ranging from being patronised to outright hostility simply for going out. The pervasiveness of deeply embedded cultural attitude around disability is revealed in the comments people routinely leave on their channel. Hannah and Shane talk about these derogatory comments that they frequently face about their unusual relationship. Shane says, "I think if people could see how boringly and horribly normal it is, that would single handedly reduce the stigma around disability if they just saw how our boring our life was"(Shane). These video blogs makes it possible for them to share their own voices, life and make themselves visible to a widespread audience at once. It is a much needed positive change as it is a unique opportunity for disabled individuals to represent their diversity and counter the commodification and elimination of interabled relationships in the dominant disability discourse.

Therefore, video blogs inarguably exist as a way to create new self images and new ways of being seen for disabled people. It is seemingly evident through this analysis that video blogs are used as an efficient political tool by disabled people to control their representation and making them more visible. They have the ability to present disability as something that is socially constructed and comprises multitude of perspectives that have the ability to challenge "narrow cultural labels that often imprison disabled people within taxonomical medical categories" (Snyder and Mitchell 194). Similar to new disability documentary cinema, video blogs by disability activists forces people to recognise constellation of experiences that inform categories of disability and to acknowledge presence of multiple existence within its boundaries (Snyder and Mitchell 194). Like Cinema, video blogs and other such mediums hold massive power in moulding society's attitudes and educating people by presenting disability in ways that promote empowerment and dislodge the widespread negative notions about disability. The above-mentioned video blogs interrogate the category of disability, influence perceptions, opinions of the viewers and increase their awareness by "unsettling the way our collective consciousness frames disability" (Thomson 1559).

As a result, visual culture studies is able to provide a rich, multi-dimensional texture to the study of disability representations while disability studies demonstrates to visual culture scholars the centrality of disability to their field. There will be no possibility of looking at the subjugated as a subject that is capable of looking back if visual culture studies is not acknowledged as a study that adds new questions and new perspectives to other disciplines. Thus, by utilising Mirzoeff's concept of "countervisuality", we can observe the potential of video blogs as a means of visual political communication for both disabled people and non disabled people. At the same time, it would be appropriate to consider video blogging as an effective weapon of resistance for the disabled and any other marginalised groups as this new way of communicating with the world leads to a transformation in the way people perceive and learn about disabilities.

Works Cited

"Anya Darlow." *YouTube*, YouTube, www.youtube.com/channel/UCCKTLefxb7XWS67U999qoRQ.

Baetens, Jan. "*The Right to Look: A Counterhistory of Visuality (review)*." Leonardo, vol. 46 no. 1, 2013, pp. 95-95.

Barnes, Colin. (1992). *Disabling imagery and the media*. Halifax, Nova Scotia: BCODP and Ryburn Publishing.

David T. Mitchell and Sharon L. Snyder, "*Representation and Its Discontents: The Uneasy Home of Disability in Literature and Film*," in The Handbook of Disability Studies Gary L. Albrecht, Katherine D. Seelman, and Michael Bury, eds. (London: Sage Publications, 2000), 198.

Davis, Lennard J., and Marquard Smith. "Editorial: Disability-Visuality." *Journal of Visual Culture*, vol. 5, no. 2, 2006, pp. 131–136., doi:10.1177/1470412906068869.

Fraser, Benjamin. *Cognitive Disability Aesthetics: Visual Culture, Disability Representations, and the (In)Visibility of Cognitive Difference*. University of Toronto Press, 2018.

Garland-Thomson, R. (1997). *Extraordinary bodies: Figuring physical disability in American culture and literature*. New York: Columbia University Press

Garland-Thomson, Rosemarie. "Integrating Disability, Transforming Feminist Theory." NWSA Journal, vol. 14, no. 3, 2002, pp. 1–32. JSTOR, JSTOR, www.jstor.org/stable/4316922.

Hevey, David. "*The Enfreakment of Photography*." The Disability Studies Reader, edited by Lennard J. Davis, Taylor & Francis, 2013, p. 432-447.

Hevey, Don. 1992. *The Creatures time forgot: photography and disability imagery*. London: Routledge.

Mirzoeff, Nicholas. *How to See the World*. Penguin Random House, 2015.

Morris, Jenny. 1993. *Pride against prejudice: transforming attitudes to disability*. London: The Women's Press.

Nicholas Mirzoeff ed., *The Visual Culture Reader*, 2nd Edition (New York: Routledge, 2007), 18.

Rosemarie Garland-Thomson, "*Feminist Disability Studies*," Signs: Journal of Women in Culture and Society 30, no. 2 (Winter 2005): 1557-1587.

Rosemarie Garland Thomson, "*The Beauty and the Freak*" Michigan Quarterly Review 37.3 (Summer 1998), 1-2.

Sharon L. Snyder And David T. Mitchell. "*Body Genres: An Anatomy of Disability in Film*." The Problem Body: Projecting Disability on Film, by Sally Chivers and Nicole Markotić, Ohio State University Press, 2010, pp. 179–207.

"Squirmy and Grubs." *YouTube*, YouTube, www.youtube.com/channel/UCdomP1JqhnyBQGaBmfDl4KQ.

3

Speaking Silence – Arguing Against Public Silence

— Prof (Dr.) Subramanian Raman Iyer

Introduction

Clarity in communication has always been the hall-mark of human relationship. When spoken words convey so much of mis-communication, how can we expect, silence to convey the correct meaning it intends to communicate. Silence can be personal silence or public silence; silence can be self-imposed or externally imposed; silence can be civil silence or criminal silence; silence can precede or succeed verbal or written communication. The meaning of silence is best understood in its context, rather than in its isolated interpretation. While the study of silence is silent on many of its dimensions, this paper limits itself to the study of public silence.

Literature Review

Generally Speaking. While different western authors have given different meaning to silence, there is no uniform interpretation to silence by Indian scholars as well. Silence can mean 'acceptance' or 'consent'; silence can mean 'indifference'; silence can mean 'submission'; silence can mean 'resistance'. Silence can threaten individual interest; silence can affect collective interest; silence may even undermine public interest. Silence is interpreted, on the one hand, as a powerful weapon by Roberts (1999). On the other, Walker (2006) supports Amartya Sen's observation that 'silence is a powerful enemy of social justice'.

Spiritually Speaking. Shankar (2014) initiates spiritual silence through two distinct steps. Spiritually speaking, physical silence through verbal withdrawal may be the beginning of mental silence towards peace and thoughtlessness. Silence is a time for physical, mental and spiritual rejuvenation. In silence, we again centre our lives and gain a fresh new perspective. When we take out time to be silent, we soon discover our true inner nature that is beyond our fluctuating mind and emotions. There is a strong case, for using silence for introspection, seeking penance and laying foundation for greater universal peace.

Socially Speaking. To express or to remain silent, may appear to be an individual choice, but what happens, when it affects the neighborhood. What happens, when it puts the community at large in jeopardy. What happens, when 'duty to speak' is silenced by the self-imposed, self-benefitting silence of majority community, to the detriment of the vulnerable minorities. Are there any examples in the history, where, such silence has abetted violence through silence, when there were compelling mandate to express opinion aloud.

Legally speaking, Silence is a state of a person, who does not speak, or of one who refrains from speaking. There are several examples in law, from Family Laws, Contract Laws, Civil Laws, Criminal Laws etc, where pure and simple silence cannot be considered as a consent, except in cases when the silent person is bound in good faith to explain himself, in which case, silence gives consent. But no assent will be inferred from a man's silence, unless, he knows his rights and knows what he is doing and his silence is voluntary.

When any person is accused of a crime, or charged with any fact, and he does not deny it, in general, the presumption is very strong that the charge is correct. The rule does not extend to the silence of a prisoner, when on his examination before a magistrate, he is charged by another prisoner with having joined him in the commission of an offence.

When an oath is administered to a witness, instead of expressly promising to keep it, he gives his assent by his silence, and kissing the book. The person to be affected by the silence must be one not disqualified to act as non compos mentis, an infant, or the like, for even the express promise of such a person would not bind him to the performance of any contract. The rule of the civil law is that silence is not an acknowledgment or denial in every case. In criminal law, especially with reference to evidence on Indian Penal Code Section 302, silence by the accused (as much as the plea guilty by the accused) is a poor evidence, for the investigating agencies.

Legal Rights to Remain Silent. The Constitution of India guarantees every person right against self incrimination under Article 20 (3): "No person accused of any offence shall be compelled to be a witness against himself". It is well established that the right to silence has been granted to the accused by virtue of the pronouncement in the case of Nandini Sathpathy vs P.L.Dani, no one can forcibly extract statements from the accused, who has the right to keep silent, but only in the court of law. It is not clear if the accused can exercise his right to silence during interrogation by public servants. Yet, the burden is on the investigating agency to prove the evidence, rather than using silence against to nail the accused.

Jurisprudence on Remaining Silent. Broadly, we can classify Silence to two major dimensions. The Civil dimensions, like consent in Marriage Acts, consent in the Contract Acts etc, where the outcome affects the civil rights of the very person exercising silence. The major aspect is the Criminal dimension, where one man's silence can be major setback to other persons' fundamental rights. How can a witness to murder remain silent, when he is the only evidence to the incident of murder?.

Before we delve deep into 'right to expression' or 'right to silence' let us examine, whether such rights are universally applicable?. If it is so universal, why is that one of the important institution of the Executive, i.e. the Armed Forces personnel, who are expected to perform their duties 'even to the peril of their life', are compelled to forgo some of their essential fundamental rights?. Article 33 & 34 empower the Parliament to restrict, modify or abrogate the fundamental rights of the members of armed forces, para-military forces, police forces, members of intelligence agencies or similar services. To ensure discipline and efficient discharge of duties by armed forces personnel, Article 33 curtails the following four fundamental rights, of such personnel:-

1. Freedom of speech.
2. Right to form associations.
3. Right to be a member of trade unions or political organizations.
4. Right to communicate with the press, and attend public meetings or demonstrations.

Here is the curb upon the law abiding Indian soldiers and their colleagues from para-military forces, but there is unfettered right to expression or unconditional right to silence, to a criminal charged with murder or sedition or even heinous crime. Generally speaking, silence has become the manipulative tool to take advantage of the legal loopholes.

Distinct Shades of Silence. There is distinct difference between self-imposed silence and the silence imposed by external environment. While law is binding upon the ordinary citizens, what about non-state players, like terrorists, who manage to silence the majority. Breaking News expression by Media and self-defined silence by people who ought to speak, call for introspection. Where is the thin-line between silence and its accountability, especially when the interest of the third-party or the common public at large, is at grave stake.

Purpose of the Study

This paper attempts to examine circumstances where there is a public duty to speak out against terrorism, violence, corrupt practices and immoral leadership, but, willy-nilly the 'neutral majority population' chooses to remain silent. This sort of 'indifferent silence' emboldens the wrong doer and results in perpetuating the crime, indefinitely.

Methodology

Analysis of case studies of 'Deliberate silence' or 'Indifferent silence' or 'Willful silence'

Case 1 – Silence during 1984 Anti-Sikh Riots

Background. By a strange turn of events in June 1984, the then Indian National Congress party in power, under Smt. Indira Gandhi, had ordered military operation 'Operation Blue Star', to clear the holy sikh shrine of Golden Temple, from the hold of the militants, who were supported by Pakistan. While the operation succeeded in clearing the terrorists from the holy shrine, some members of the sikh community felt alienated due to military operations inside their holy shrine. This had led to the unfortunate incident of Smt. Indira Gandhi, getting gunned down by her own sikh body-guards, on 31 October, 1984. As the assailants were from the Sikh community, there was a massive communal backlash upon the innocent sikh community members, in Delhi and other parts of the Country. The ruling *Indian National Congress* had been in active complicity with the mob. Independent sources estimated the number of deaths at about 8,000–17,000 whilst government estimates projected that about 2,800 Sikhs were killed in Delhi and 3,350 nationwide.

Silence of Congress Party and Delhi Police. After the 1984 anti-Sikh riots, the then Congress government's silence was unrepentant. The statement of Rajiv Gandhi itself was very shameless. Commenting on the anti-Sikh riots in Delhi, Rajiv

Gandhi said, "When a giant tree falls, the earth below shakes"; a statement for which he was widely criticized. Many Congress politicians were accused of orchestrating the violence. But the Congress leaders were shamelessly propagating it. This was mean and hateful. Instead of healing the wounds (of the victims), they were rubbing salt. This was emotionless and inhuman.

Judicial Condemnation of on Public Silence. The silence of Delhi Police during the 1984 anti-Sikh riots was a 'serious lapse' on its part and it appeared to be 'privy' in the incidents of rioting, an Indian court has said. District and Sessions Judge J R Aryan said that as per the report of Justice G T Nanavati Commission, 341 persons were killed in Delhi Cantonment area during the riots. In the case relating to it, Congress leader Sajjan Kumar has been acquitted. But, as per the record of Palam Colony police station, 'not a single incident of killing was recorded by the police', the court noted. 'From the evidence and material available in this case,...these facts and circumstances do suggest that law supervising and enforcing machinery i.e.(Delhi) police maintained complete silence during those two days i.e. November 1 and 2, 1984', the court, in its judgement, said. Court can take judicial notice of the fact available from Justice Nanavati Commission report that there were as many 341 killings in police station Delhi Cantt. area itself and the present case concerning killing of five persons was in the area of Rajnagar, Palam colony, a part of police station Delhi Cantt. 'It has come in evidence from document, the DDR, maintained at police station Palam Colony, that not a single incident of any killing or any property destroyed was recorded by the police,' it said. During the arguments, CBI had contended there was a conspiracy of 'terrifying proportion' between Sajjan Kumar and the Delhi Police during the riots. The agency had said the police had kept its 'eyes closed' to the widespread violence. The court also agreed with the arguments of CBI that 'police appeared to be privy in the incidents of rioting may be by maintaining their status as silent spectator'

Eapen (2016) states that not only the Congress Government and the Delhi Police who remained silent, but the common citizens, who could have prevented the escalation of violence, remained silent. The neighbours, government servants, religious teachers etc, remained criminally silent. This public silence subsequently led to serious alienation among the sikh community members. The wounds took long to heal.

Case 2 : Silence of Common J & K Muslims When Terrorists Resorted to Ethnic cleansing of Hindus

Background. In the early Nineties, the Pakistan sponsored militancy in Jammu and Kashmir was at its peak. The common Kashmiris were sandwiched, between the peace loving India and war-mongering Pakistan. Pakistan's evil plans to bleed India, through thousand cuts (as a revenge for Indian support to the independence of East Pakistan as Bangla Desh in 1971), left the common Kashmiri voiceless. Suddenly, in 1990, the militancy took a religious tone, leading to ethnic cleansing of Hindus out of the Kahmir Valley. The odds were against the common Kashmiris, both Hindus and Muslims alike. But when some majority Muslim community, joined hands with the Pakistani militants to drive away their Hindu brethren and neighbours, centuries of communal harmony came crashing down in Kashmir. Not only some abetted the militants, many remained silent to this date.

Sample Voice of a Silenced Kashmiri Hindu - Aarti Tikoo Singh – A Narration

"I'm no more an outsider in Kashmir -With its diversity of ethnicities and religious communities, Jammu and Kashmir has been nothing but a microcosm of plural India. That was during and till the early 1980s when Kashmiris —Hindus, Muslims and Sikhs — prayed and lived peacefully in shared spaces. My father and his Muslim friends grew up at each other's homes in the 1950s and 1960s. After my grandparents and parents, aapa and abbu, who performed namaz five times a day, were my guardians.

By the end of 1989, all of it had unraveled— the Pandit community's most prolific writer and lawyer in the small town where we lived was shot dead; more than 20 Pandits were killed by the Pakistan-backed Islamist insurgents in Kashmir in a month. Muslims, especially girls from Hindu community, were ordered to follow Islamic dress code. On the morning of the New Year 1990, the decree on our banishment from the Kashmir Valley was issued by JKLF on its letterhead and pasted on our gate. On January 19, 1990, hordes of separatists in mosques and streets blared communal slogans while evoking "Nizam-e-Mustafa", "Pakistan" and "azadi" (from India).

Ten days later, our parents put us in a truck along with other neighbourhood girls, and sent us 300 km away from Kashmir. By the end of 1990, the exodus of Kashmiri Pandits from the Valley was complete. Part of my family ended up in refugee camps while we grew up in rented pigeonholes of Jammu, the Hindu-dominated region, which was ethnically, linguistically and culturally completely different from Kashmir. Our parents insisted that we stayed in the camps with our family members during school vacations. Uprooted and disenfranchised, the community for the sake of survival sold ancestral properties in Kashmir for peanuts and attempted to assimilate in the rich diversity and vastness of India. Many Pandit women married outside the community and lost the state subject rights of Jammu & Kashmir permanently until 2002 when the J&K High Court restored their rights. But none of the women could pass on their rights to their children and spouses.

I began visiting Kashmir as a journalist from 2002 — the Valley that I had grown up had changed completely. The fringe — separatists and militants — were the most vocal section while the ordinary Kashmiri had been silenced and coerced into toeing their line. Hundreds of civilians had been killed for standing up for India. On gunpoint, the separatists had managed to dictate the narrative and the storyline. Kashmir was under siege but neither New Delhi nor anyone else in India could rescue its common people.I was an 'outsider' in my own Kashmir home; I stopped mentioning my surname in Kashmir. On my professional visits,

I was a journalist and on personal, I was merely a tourist. There was bloodshed all around; heartbreaking stories of orphans who had lost their parents to the violence and wailing mothers whose sons never returned home. Assignments during each crisis in Kashmir was always like reliving heartache and grief of every Kashmiri person.

Though the Articles were supposedly inserted in the Constitution to protect the state's distinct identity, few were asked what its identity was to begin with. With its diversity of ethnicities and religious communities, Jammu and Kashmir has been nothing but a microcosm of plural India. Within Kashmir, what we repeatedly call 'Kashmiryat' was the syncretic culture and identity that Hindus, Muslims and Sikhs had created through hundreds of years together. In other words, Kashmir is the idea of India and India is the idea of Kashmir our ancestors nourished.

But in the last 30 years, the exclusivist identity — the idea of a two nation theory, which India rejected in 1947, had been allowed to grow in Kashmir. When the Centre announced that it had reorganised the state and thus brought down the walls that had been erected between communities I asked myself: am I still an outsider in Kashmir? I looked around and wondered if my homecoming was happening at the expense of somebody else's sense of identity. I wasn't sure how to feel. I had given up on home in Kashmir long ago, seeing how the violent fringe dominated the perception not just in the Valley but also in New Delhi. But the unthinkable had happened.

Later in the afternoon, while having Kashmiri tea at the home of a friend who practices the Islam of Nund Rishi, the patron Sufi saint of Kashmir, I heard him addressing my unexpressed thoughts: "You may think the entire Valley is angry with the decision. Trust me, most are heaving a sigh of relief. We are silent because we have been silenced by fear for 30 years. Let the guns and violence on the streets end and you will see all of us share the same identity as we have always had for hundreds of years".

Case 3: Silence by Majority Sinhalese community, when brutal violence was perpetuated against Common Tamils in Sri Lanka

Muted Voice of the Tamil Victims. Most of the majority knows what is happening, but are silent. So long as something does not affect them, they remain apathetic. If the majority Singhalese really cared why did they (the majority) remain silent when Tamil civilians were getting bombed in the no fire zones?

Why don't they ask for an impartial inquiry into what happened in the last days of the war? Why did they remain silent and not raise a voice about the appalling conditions the Tamils had to suffer in the so called welfare camps? Why were there no protests when Tamils were being abducted in white vans? Why no protests when the Government of Sri Lanka is dragging its feet on implementing the 'Lesson Learnt and Reconciliation Commission report and holding elections in the North? Why no protests when the Uthayan newspapers was burned to the ground?.

Most of them are too busy making ends meet, while the rest just don't care. Most of them will tell you that we are all brothers and sisters under one flag…that we are one country, one people and one nation…but in their hearts almost all of them believe in the Mahavamsa myth of this country belonging only to the Sinhala Buddhists.

This is the reason for their silence and complicity in everything that has been happening post war. The Rajapaksas' are playing the race card for votes because they know that a majority of the majority are either openly racist, closet racists or just "we don't care what happens as long as we are safe Sinhala Buddhists."

Years after the end of Sri Lanka's long and bloody civil war, a "silent" conflict is being waged across the island, with tens of thousands of government troops continuing to occupy the north and east and the army expanding its property developments on land belonging to displaced Tamils, a new report claims.

Results and Discussion

The above three case studies are simply representative case studies of Public silence, bearing close similarities, both in context and consequences, There are hundred other case studies world over, who bear close resemblance to these cases. What stands distinct from the point of view of 'Public Silence' stands highlighted in this study.

Anti-Sikh Riots of 1984. In the case of Anti-Sikh riots of 1984, the minority Sikhs were singled out. The majority community could have expressed their solidarity and protected them, but failed to do so. This has emboldened the criminals and street-ruffians, to perpetuate greater violence upon the innocents. There was neither physical support against, to prevent the violence, nor emotional support to assuage the consequences of the macabre targeted violence. There was no case of any Congressman/Public members, voicing their concern, to stop the violence, both during the violence, or thereafter. In fact, there was a justifiable tone, in support of the violence, rather than repentance or regret. Public silence by Political parties, Government machineries, intelligentsia and media personnel added fuel to the mob, that indulged in the violence.

Ethnic Cleansing of Hindus from Jammu and Kashmir. The situation was worst in the ethnic cleansing of Hindus from Jammu and Kashmir. Those who lived harmoniously for generations, became helpless overnight. In a hostile militancy environment, we understand that the population is divided into three distinct segments. (1) those supporting the militants, (2) those opposing militants and (3) the neutral majority. In the case of Jammu and Kashmir, the neutral Muslim majority, showed greater affinity to the Pakistan militants due to their religious ethnicity and due to their misplaced loyalty to Pakistan, at the cost of their Hindu brethren, who lived beside them for generations. It is ironic that no Kashmiri political leaders, vocally condemned the terrorists, for their heinous crimes, nor got killed for speaking the truth. Even common people and media, remained 'Publicly Silent', when they had a duty to express their solidarity with the hapless Hindu neighbour. Large number of Hindu families moved out of their native homes, and lived their rest of the life in migrant camps, temples, Gurudwara etc. When sporadic efforts were made by the Governments to rehabilitate these migrants, back in their native Kashmiri homes, the terrorists resisted it violently and the common Kashmiri Muslims abetted to it, conveniently. How could some of them ignore the advantage they got from the landed properties, left behind by the Hindu migrants in abject distress. Even today, after the legal expiry of Article 370, there is no welcome calls from the moderate Muslims in Kashmir to their erstwhile neighbor, to get back to Kashmir.

How do we interpret the present situation in Kashmir?. Is it a case of 'Deliberate silence' as was the case in the past, or is it a case of 'Wilful Silence' to impede the process of normalcy. Who stands to gain from such a Public silence?. The onus of restoring the normalcy, now lies upon the common Kashmiri, to speak out; yes to speak out loudly, so that truth gets its rightful support. No amount of developmental works, no amount of political reconciliation, no amount of social integration of Kashmir with rest of India, will happen, until the 'roar of the Silence' is heard loud and clear, in verbal expression, world over. Until then normalcy will continue to elude people of Kashmir.

Voiceless Tamils of Sri Lanka. Without going into the details of the civil war, that lasted for more than three decades, and its final phase, where disproportionate force was used to against the common Tamils, I will only highlight the aspect of public silence of the Sinhalese majority. Everyone knows it well that the LTTE (Liberation Tigers of Tamil Eelam) and Sri Lanka Army, were engaged in a bloody conflict till May 2009. Without going into the righteousness of the military operation, my comments will stand limited to 'petrified Silencing of the common Tamils, and willful public silence of the Singhalese.. Hundreds of Tamils were killed under suspicious circumstances; thousands of them were detained in detention camps; more than a million Tamil population was displaced out of their native homes, for several years, after the conflict. There was no sympathy, no compassion from their fellow Sinhalese citizens. Several international probing agencies, have come out in support of common Tamil population, but there was a 'muted Silence' from the Sinhalese population. Even today, the plight of the common Tamil population, has not improved. There is no significant efforts from the common Singhalese citizens to integrate the marginalized Tamil population, into the main stream. The situation is alarmingly silent, publicly silent, to a point of sowing the seeds for the next level of violence. Remember, when injustice can not be silenced for too long.

Conclusion

If there can be regret by the British Prime Minister for 'Jalia Wala Bagh massacre', if there can be regret by Japanese Prime Minister for war-crimes during Second World War, is there not a case for reconciliation in Sri Lanka, Punjab or Jammu and Kashmir. Can the majority Sinhalese break their public silence, and come out in support of the common Tamils, atleast for the sack of posterity. Can the majority Muslims in Kashmir speak up against terrorism and welcome their Hindu neighbour with open arms? Is there not a case for asking forgiveness, for the anti-sikh riots by those, suspected to be involved in it?

For long, armament and atom bombs, have divided the nations and people. Economic and Political powers have taken centre-stage. Is there not a case for greater people to people relationship through communication. When there is a public duty to speak, there is no escape from speaking. Ignoring this duty to speak, amounts to tacit support to violent forces. There is a powerful weapon system with every citizen. i.e. the right to speak. The right to speak for righteousness, is the need of the hour. Therefore, I call upon the people to discern the context correctly and speak up; publicly speak up and burst out their self imposed Public silence.

Works Cited

Dowling, A. (1995). "The Other Side of Silence": Matrimonial Conflict and the Divorce Court in George Eliot's Fiction. *NINETEEN CENT LIT, 50*(3), 322-336.

Eapen, P.G. (2017), *The Silence of Many: The Fallout of Operation Blue Star,* Viva Books Private Limited, New Delhi ISBN: 978-81-309-3100-5.

Finley, L. M. (1989). "Breaking women's silence in law: The dilemma of the gendered nature of legal reasoning". *Notre Dame L. Rev., 64,* 886.

https://www.news18.com/news/politics/congress-rubbing-salt-on-wounds-of-1984-anti-sikh-riots-victims-aap-1283592.html accessed on 15 Oct 19.

https://www.indiatoday.in/india/story/silence-of-delhi-police-during-1984-riots-was-a-serious-lapse-says-court-161419-2013-05-01 accessed on 20 Oct 19.

https://economictimes.indiatimes.com/articleshow/70623004.cms?from=mdr&utm_source=contentofinterest&utm_medium=text&utm_campaign=cppst accessed on 10 Oct 19.

https://www.theguardian.com/global-development/2015/may/28/sri-lanka-army-land-grabs-tamil-displacement-report-oakland-institute accessed on 12 Oct 19.

Menikoff, J. (1998). "Doubts about death: the silence of the Institute of Medicine". *The Journal of Law, Medicine & Ethics, 26*(2), 157-165.

Roberts, D. E. (1999). "The paradox of silence: Some questions about silence as resistance". *U. Mich. JL Reform, 33,* 343.

Shankar, S. S. R. (2014). *Celebrating Silence.* Arktos.

Walker, M. (2006). "Towards a capability-based theory of social justice for education policy-making". *Journal of Education Policy, 21*(2), 163-185.

4

Exploring Silence as a Feminist Strategy: An Indian Perspective in Shashi Deshpande's *That Long Silence*

— *Dr Shweta Sengar*

This paper tries to explore feminist strategy in the leading text of Shashi Deshpande's *That Long Silence* and comes out with the conclusion that feminist strategies refer to reading & writing practices grounded in women's experiences.

The findings revels that universal texts are permeated with prejudices toward women & need to be interpreted from feminist perspective some of the most important general questions that are probed into are: Whose experience is rendered most fully and faithfully in literacy texts? Is this a novel that represents women's experience from the inside, sympathetically, as the same of the women as someone evolving with some inner freedom or choice? At the same time, are women presented as stereotypes (the alluring mistress, the dominating bitch, the all providing earth mother)? Are women seen locked into patterns, with no significant freedom or flexibility? Is there hidden misogyny or overt misogyny? Are masculine & feminine activities and values presented differently? Another set of questions has to do with how the author presents the society she is setting the work in, & the ideology of that society.

A third set of questions was about how the reader or the narrator is "constructed" I the text. This novel gives explicit specifications about what kind of reader they are soliciting, & the readers fit in with those specifications, or resist them, & find themselves reading against the grain of the novel. A final set of questions are: whose desires & fantasies are driving the novel? when it comes to an end, does the feeling of confliction come from the fact that someone's desires have been achieved? The feminist strategy that come into being was silence. Shashi Deshpande's *That Long Silence* is written in the first person narrative. The first person narrator, Jaya, is the female protagonist of the novel who undergoes harrowing experiences in her marital life. Right from the very beginning of the narrative Jaya suffers from a state of spiritual or mental division due to conflicting impulses: she fails to make a choice between her creative urge as a writer and her duty as a faithful and devoted wife. The whole narrative is nothing but her quest for identity or the search for the self. That Long Silence is an exceptionally accomplished portrayal of a woman trying to erase a 'long silence' begun in childhood and rooted in herself and in the constraints of her life. This novel can be taken as a genre in confessional mode in which the protagonist of the novel lays bare her soul and the wound inflicted on her by the patriarchal setup. Throughout her narrative Jaya ruminates over her past which is full of failure and frustration on every front of her life. It takes the form of her candid confession because of the patriarchal constraints. The novel outlines the predicament of a woman in a male dominated society, the problems that she faces in defining herself and attaining an autonomous selfhood. It also establishes the fact that Jaya is victim of unjust social discrimination. The title of the novel that is taken from a speech of Elizabeth Robins and is quite appropriate in that it suggests the predicament of a woman in patriarchal society who silently suffers the humiliation and subjugation. Jaya seldom gets a chance to realize her true self. The division that she suffers from is because of her divided loyalty between the creative writer and the housewife sparing no efforts in pleasing her husband and locking after her children. The only conviction with which she had been living for full seventeen years is the innate faith that it is more important to be good wife than a good writer. This feeling at least gave her "The illusion of happiness".

Shashi Deshpande's woman protagonist Jaya has used silence as a literary strategy. The existential angst of Jaya (Chapter VI) being when she finds her familiar existence disrupted, her husband's reputation in question and their future as a family in jeopardy. What pricks her most is the consciousness of being a failure as a writer. She is haunted by memories of the past. Differences with her husband, frustration in their seventeen –year-old marriage, disappointment in her two teenage children, and claustrophia of her childhood – all being to surface. In her small suburban Bombay flat, Jaya ceaselessly grapples with some bitter truths about herself.

When she is finally settled emotionally, she pens down all her suppressed feelings and suffering that she underwent in her seventeen years of silence. It is by penning her story, her fears, her doubts and anguish that she has been able to articulate her predicament and break her silence. The drudgery of the household, and entertaining her husband's quests, she does not have any say in it thus denying any space deserved in her own right first insight that she gains in her silence is that," I'm not afraid any more. The panic has gone; I'm Mohan's wife. I had thought, and cut off the bits of me that had refused to be Mohan's wife. Now I know that kind of fragmentation is not possible" (191). The second realization that comes to her is that life is to be lived fully in relationship with others and decides that she shall not be passive and silent any more. She plans to live life "whole" life, retaining all that did not fit in the straitjacket of "wifehood". She has decided that she would not look in Mohan's face for clues and then give him "the answer I know he wants". This decision fills her with vigor and buoyancy. She believes that one cannot live in fragments. In the final sage Jaya emerges as a person divested of all self-deception and artificialities that she has all long been living with Jaya battles against authoritarian and male hegemonic discourse & is determined to "dare to live the life she imagines" "Society attacks anyone who dares to say its wins are counterfeit, but when it is a women who says this, society begins to foam at the month. It puts aside all its theories and arguments picks up the women of felt to fling at her" The female protagonist Jaya as her name symbolizes victory raises her voice against traditions & social norms. Few male writes depict the woes & pains of women the way a women writer does. Kate Millet points out that one of the most potent & powerful institution of patriarchy is family & its affects "control & conformity" (sexual politics 55) Despite her ceaseless efforts in looking after the family, rearing up the children, doing all the dreary.

At the end of the novel Jaya's husband loses his confidence, his position as an engineer. In the unbar & global society her husband becomes the victim & correction. During the seventeen yrs of marriage Mohan never asks her opinion on any matter but when an inquiry has been set up against, him he holds Jaya's hands and asks her to supports the family through her career as a writer. But Jaya remains silent. This is a kind of protest against her long silence, which makes her strong at the end of the novel.

Works Cited

Bartky, Sandra L. (1990). *Femininity and Domination: Studies in the Phenomenology of Oppression*. London: Routledge.

Beauvoir, Simone de, *The Second Sex*. Trans. H. M. Parshley. Repr. New York: Vintage, 1971. (Ist French Edition, 1949).

Deshpande, Shashi, *That Long Silence*. New Delhi: Penguin, 1989.

Ellman, Mary. *Thinking about Women*, New York: Harcourt Brace Jovanovich, 1968.

Emerson, Ralph Waldo. 'Self - Reliance'. In William H. Gilman. Ed. *Selected Writings of Ralph Waldo Emerson*. New York, 1962, pp 254 - 270.

Firestone, Shulamith. *The Dialectic of Sex: the Case of Feminist Revolution*. New York: William Morrow and Company, 1971.

Freund, E. *The Return of the Reader: Reader* - Response criticism, London: Methuen, 1987.

Fuss, D. *Essentially Speaking: Feminism, Nature and difference*, London: Rutledge, 1989.

Iyengar, KR Srinivas. *Indian Writing in English*. New Delhi: Sterling Publishers, 1999.

Part - III

Silence and the Subaltern Consciousness

1

History's Phantom Limb: Re-Membering the Devadasis of Kochi

— *Priya V.*

"There have been no devadasis in Kerala. It is possible to speak about them only if such a custom was in practice anywhere in Kerala, which has never been the case." — **Kavalam Narayana Panikkar**

"The kind of royal centres, massive temples and temple urbanity that evolved in the rest of South India did not emerge in Kerala. Consequently, the devadasi system too has never been in existence here." — **P. Soman**

"Remembering is never quite an act of introspection. It is a... re-membering, a putting together of the dis-membered past ..." — **Homi Bhabha**

The objective of my paper is drawn from a melding of unexplored archival documents and ethnographic research which consists in an investigation of linkages between the construction of Kochi's emerging modernity and the production and dissemination of the idea of regression, evincing a visceral sense of cultural dirt as selectively applied to the social and sexual practices of devadasis and their consequent displacement from popularly acknowledged pasts. Against the backdrop of the forced absence of references to devadasis from the official histories and cultural common sense of

Kerala, what I seek to understand is how metaphorical phantom-limbs of history are created precisely to evoke the sanctity of a region's legitimate past.

I can only claim a partial foothold among the by now rich arena of scholarly works that has tackled various kinds of invisibilities by tapping up memories accessed through oral narrations otherwise marginalized in mainstream histories. I channel critical interest rather to the fragmentary dynamics of remembering that I encountered in my ethnographic research, to scraps of remembered pasts activated in the absence of tactile connections to bodily memories a hereditary repertory can invigorate. This evocation of the fragment has less to do with the researcher's postmodern commitment and more with her own discomfort stemming from her personal engagement with the lacunae that characterize commemorative attempts by descendants of devadasis in their current reconstitution in patriarchal, "postmemory" contemporariness marked by multi-generational distance and creative mediation in the face of wrenching displacements and social stigma (Hirsch 1997).

The earliest bunch of the archival documents I have been able to locate, a totally unexplored relic from a forgotten past pertaining to the devadasis of Kochi, dates from 1933 and consists in a few letters exchanged between various authorities of the dyarchic Kochi state regarding the adoption of a girl named, Manikkyam by a 'First House Devadasi', Meenakshi Draupadi at the Gosripuresa temple of the multilingual Konkani community in Mattanchery. The letter from the Diwan's Secretary states that, since "the evils attendant on the institution of the Devadasis are well known", there is a need to address "the larger question" regarding "the probable purpose for which such adoptions take place" which "should be recognized by the government as a matter of public policy" (*Huzur Secretariat Files* 1933). Translating moral discomfort as rational assessment, this letter seems to have already settled the matter, bracketing it within the obviousness of common knowledge.

The 'public' that seeks a complete ban of the custom has various representatives, they self-consciously figure in their deliberations as negotiators of modernity and cultural reformism. A major investment in this direction towards a final ban was largely the work of the male members of the devadasi community itself. The Cochin Saraswath Association as a result was established in 1938. S. Padmanabha, who had spearheaded the Association's various efforts towards a complete ban of the custom complains that following the sanctioning of voluntary dancing by the King, "some old devadasis are dancing and singing in the temple violating the Government order dated 18-10-41" (*Huzur Secretariat Files* 1942). The representation thus brought to the King however, was countered by a complaint filed by the devadasis themselves on 29th January, 1942 under the name of a performer named Gangi Lakshmi.

We learn from the Secretary's Report from the previous year that a petition was filed by Gangi Laxmi earlier on 2nd October, 1939 signed by 44 of the total 50 performing women dedicated at the temple. I have not been able to locate this earlier petition; the second petition dated 29th January, 1942, is all we have and it is an impassioned representation of their collective identities as paid artists working in a religious ambience. This petition again announces the petitioner with her official designation (Gangi Laxmi, 1st House Devadasi, Palace Road, Cochin) and seeks the intervention of the king to redress their grievances. It mentions how emoluments amounting to more than 600 rupees for the various services rendered by them at the temple for over two and a half years have been withheld irrespective of three petitions filed by them and that they continue to be "humiliated and insulted when we go to the temple for voluntary worship or perquisites" and that on one occasion "a Police Head-Constable in the presence of hundreds of people assembled in the spot, insulted and threatened us and even assaulted one of us" (Lakshmi 1942). The petition may only afford only a shred of insight to the resistance put in by a collective of devadasis against the steadily building tides of moral reform, and yet somewhere among the missed documents, "the discontinuities that offer history" as Foucault puts it, linger the afterlives of the women who had fought to have their voices heard and restore the dignity that was suddenly wrenched from them (10).

To bring into frame the kind of opinion building within Kochi's emergent public sphere that vitiated devadasis asprostitutes we need to turn from the controlled registers of bureaucratic legalese to works in popular media by the most vociferous among the custom's attackers, M. R. Nair, popularly known as Sanjayan. However, we need to go back in time here, to 1927 to reconstruct the roles of particular historical agents, the actor in question here being no less a persona than Mahatma Gandhi. While addressing a crowd in Ernakulum on 13th October 1927, Gandhi asks if they could cite "any justification of the deplorable devadasi custom" (Nair 352). An unidentified voice from the crowd answers that "there are no native devadasis here, they have been imported from outside" (352). Gandhian rhetoric here accomplishes a masterstroke as he situates persistence of devadasi practices within a region as a matter of collective shame: "Even if there was only one devadasi left, it was a huge shame to all youth" (352).

The nub of the matter here is that the discourse of reform within colonial modernity also set the normative example of patrifocal family and monogamic marriage, from the purview of which the kind of female adoption that often sustained the practices of temple women could no longer fit in the familial mode projected at once as a rational and moral norm. Construction of otherness consisting in the idea of non-belonging attached to the performers is thus predicated on a nation-wide opinion-building through the discourse of regression or deplorability projected on to them and penalizing their practices.

Sanjayan's writings published in the *Viswaroopam* in the early 1940s consistently vilify the devadasis whom he calls *tevidissis* (a term which has emerged as a common cuss word for women suggesting a fallen status) through acerbic moralizing and collation of their dance with prostitution. It would be insightful to connect his critique with a cartoon under the name of M. Bhaskaran that was featured in *Viswaroopam* in 1941. The cartoon features a beautiful woman dancing to the accompaniment of musicians. On the folds of her flowing skirt are printed the words: 'devadasi dance renaissance' while a man with a flashy grin is shown walking towards her with open arms from the background. In the front row, we find seated, poet Vallathol Narayana Menon, who is enthusiastically gesticulating to the beauty of the dance. The caption given to the cartoon goes thus: "It is pathetic that, in his eagerness to congratulate the Government of Kochi for re-introducing *dasiyaattam*, Mahakavi Vallathol failed to see the lecher who the Mahakavi himself had written about in 'Kochu Sita', and stands secretly behind every devadasi" (Bhaskaran 150). The remarkable power of this cartoon consists in the fact that by framing alternative perceptions of the custom within the shameless emblems of a pre-modern provincial state, it forecloses possibilities of other respectable takes on the same whereby anyone who might regard the dance otherwise, naturally becomes inevitably immoral and regressive.

The jibe directed at Vallathol draws from the fact that in a speech published in the *Mathrubhoomi* daily on November 30th, 1940, the poet directed attention to the remarkable beauty of the dance of Kochi's devadasis and went on to claim that given a choice between art and morality, he would opt the former. Sanjayan's rejoinder to Vallathol's position on the issue takes the shape of an acidic tirade when he elaborates thus: "The great poet has uncovered himself as a sycophant in his decision to support the Kochi Government's latest step to re-introduce *dasiyattam* in the temples of Cochin, which many great men all over India has put down as totally shameless and disgusting" (174). Invoking the larger nation-wide background where concerted efforts to ban the custom were already in place Sanjayan unleashes his moral indignation thus:

> Isn't it true that if an assessment regarding what percentage of art and morality has a place in the life of devadasis is made,

> the notorious truth that ninety-eight percent of their income is drawn from prostitution, as against art, will be arrived at? To promote and uplift this meagre two percent of art would he parade the decayed smelly corpse of the devadasi custom, emitting the stench of dead morality back to the temple premises? Can't it be taught at centres of art instituted for the same purpose, to girls from respectable families who don't need to earn their livelihood from prostitution.... Seems there is art in their dance! Isn't there art in some songs sung at a toddy shop? Or in the way an expert butcher wields his knife as he performs his trade? Or in the lust-ridden glances, seductive gaits and mock-anger of the *tevidissi* adept in the arts of Kama? Will the great poet allow relaxation also in accepting the said *tevidissi* along with her art? ......The rose-bush of art is not to be cultivated by uprooting the wholesome grain-bearing stalks of morality. We would recommend that the hand that attempts the same, no matter of a great poet, must necessarily be hacked away (174-175).

Here we have, I would contend, as in the alien alterity attributed to devadasis in the interactions between Gandhi and a Malayali audience, the articulation of a major phantom-limb of Kerala's legitimate history, a discursive amputating act that is possible only since nation-wide penalization procedures and reformism campaigns were already on the roll. This argument finds graphic illustration in a caricature in the same issue of *Viswaroopam.* Captioned 'Father and Daughter!!', the caricatured scenario presents the land of Kerala personified as a beautiful young woman named Kairali handing over her baby girl, 'Kochu Sita' to its father Vallathol. Valllathol's public acknowledgement that he would choose art over morality is caricatured here by making him the 'illegitimate' father of the devadasi born to Kairali.

I collate a bricolage of four more cartoons by the same artist who had caricatured devadasis' performance practices to foreground the kind of latent tensions and assumed standards of gender behaviour underplaying *Viswaroopam*'s clamour for reforms. Constructed within imagined polarities of 'Then' and 'Now', the caricatures portend a dismal future, where following women's entry into various public spaces, a cataclysmic reversal of what is projected as 'natural' gender behaviour gets to be intuited leading up to emasculation of men and sexual anarchy. All these visceral fears converge, for the 'culturally minded' writers and artists of *Viswaroopam*, in the practices of this small community of devadasis who could now be defiled as Kerala's illegal progeny, in whose case the inner and the outer, the material and the spiritual, home and the world seem to be seamlessly merged. To examine how the visuality of dance bridges colonial modernity's conceptualizations of the public and the private domain, I drive critical interest away from Partha Chatterjee's extremely influential argument about the separation of public and private domains within the nationalist debate towards Tithi Bhattacharya's insightful consideration that the two spheres may not have been as scrupulously discrete as is read by Chatterjee in his contention that nationalism began its journey after it had already proclaimed its sovereignty in the inner domain (Bhattacharya 921, Chatterjee 10). Bhattacharya instead diverts attention to the entanglements of private and public domains to study how the highly gendered language of nationalism "linked the emergent public sphere of modern political discourse to the sphere of private and domestic practices, thereby reconstituting both" (921). Hence, the female body that can be a repository of legitimate art in the public eye of Kochi's incipient modernity must necessarily be a receptacle of chastity!

In a pamphlet that I have been able to locate circulated among the devadasis of Kochi in 1940, they are exhorted "to wake up and restore their lost dignity" and "to enable the great nation of India to hold its head high among other countries by completely wiping off a custom that blots the face of Indian womanhood!" Ironically, the respect the devadasis are exhorted to wholeheartedly embrace is an ideal entrenched in the Janus-faced instincts of colonial modernity, the scripting of which can legitimize itself only within the slate-cleaning gestures of re-written pasts. It is hence that I would contend, we need to rephrase Antoinette Burton's definition of colonial modernities' efforts as 'an unfinished business', to be also a patently paradoxical project (1-16).

And yet, a hauntological reactivation of the missed possibilities of history points to stories evacuated from a people's collective memory. None of these acts of individual memory can be said to be wholesome. But right in their sketchy shapes, when pooled together, they conjure up other versions of elided pasts. The first of these from the autobiography of poet, G. Sankarakurup presents an ekphrastic description of the rich sentient appeal among the masses and allure of the dance of Kochi's devadasis at the Poornathrayesa temple, the abode of the royal family's patron deity, inviting the remonstrance of his teacher and hence ends with a lamentation of the 'degeneration' of its performers. The second, drawn from an oral reminiscence of the dance watched by an octogenarian Brahmin historian of the Konkani community named Purushothama Mallaya relates routine ritualistic performances by *dasis* at the Gosripuresa temple from older times. Following the typical trope of erstwhile sanctity and later degeneration assumed in nationalist historiography he went on to claim that the caste name, Saraswath Non-brahmins adopted by the community following legal banning of the custom in 1936 is not acceptable, as according to him, it is not possible to be Saraswath and claim backward caste status at the same time. My third informant, a former official at the palace of the last Kochi king, recollected the dance of the *dasis* he had watched as a major insignia of Kochi's regal splendour and went on to distinguish it from Mohiniyattam patronised at the Thiruvitaamkoor court which he insisted was a synonym for prostitution.The relationalities constructed in these narratives, always fixed against something else, emerge as strong anchors for their characterization. Vague memories of the dance of the *dasis* in the very popular *Athachamayam* procession in Kochi during Onam, at least until 1942 survive among the descendants of the community that I interacted with. As an annual performative act that relaxes caste norms otherwise stringently followed, the procession was a cartographic attempt to stage royal power, a shrewd appropriation of the mythical return of the legendary king Mahabali to act out royal power. While earlier editions of State Encyclopaedias do mention the performance of devadasis in the royal procession, they are elided in later editions as a redundant fact. Current nostalgic representations of the old enchantment of the procession recycled every year during the festive season typically would contain no mention of the same. It is as if we have also forgotten the fact that we have forgotten. Female descendants of the erstwhile performers talked about the *bahumanam* (respect) the performers once claimed, one of them, a sprightly sixty-eight-year-old, Renuka who sells milk and *papadams* from her two room home struck out experiential affiliations with devadasis elsewhere and went on to mention celebrated musician from a devadasi lineage, M. S. Subbulakshmi. Remembering becomes a survival mechanism here. She further pointed out how birth, marital and funeral ceremonies in the community are now identical to that of Gowda Saraswath Brahmins. "*Vyathyasam*" (difference) she insists was created, "I attach no meaning to it" (Bai 2013). In the front veranda of her home, mounted on the wall among black and white pictures was a wedding certificate that declared she and her late husband to be legally wedded, a common practice, I was told, among older women of the community. Difference is translated into staged sameness so that it fits modernity's normative blueprint for respectable citizenship, in effect naturalizing the patrifocal monogamic family. None of the women I talked with could speak of the repertory of their ancestors; Renuka only mumbled "everything's gone, nobody remembers anything", "youngsters do not like to listen to us talking about old times, may be a couple of generations down they will forget this disgrace as well", she hoped (Bai 2013).

The world of devadasis re-membered in Renuka's reminiscing is a world dead and gone, a *memento mori* thatlies buried under the verbal overlay of experienced stigma which refuses to disappear. And yet, the conscientious individual can play with its atomizing effects through imaginative re-creations of her past, clearing space within herself for the subject's own plurality because the screens that inflect looking as they are historically generated can be played with for the same reason, blurring the lines between approximation to convention and possible resistance to the same. It is hence that imaginative acts of commemoration in postmemory can also fitfully become a "rememoration" and resistance against organized forgetting and persistent stigma (Hirsch 256). I stop short of celebratory enunciations of counter memory here in the hope that scholarly ambition does not add up to the antinomies spawned in historical accounts of progress, perhaps it is enough to direct attention to "the play of power in the labour of difference" and "the place of difference in the work of power" (Dube 89).

Works Cited

Bai, Renuka. Personal Interview. 30 Mar. 2013.

Bhabha, Homi K. *The Location of Culture*. London, New York: Routledge, 1994. Print.

Bhaskaran, M. "Annum Innum!" *Viswaroopam*. 1.6 (1941): 155. Print.

---. "Devadasi Nritha Punarudharanam." Cartoon. *Viswaroopam*. 1.6 (1941): 150.

Print.

---. "Paattu Poya Pokku!!" Cartoon. *Viswaroopam*. 1.3 (1940): 7. Print.

---. "Misravidyabhyasathinte Purogathi." Cartoon. *Viswaroopam*. 1.3 (1940): 11.

Print.

---. "Vivahalochana: Annum Innum." Cartoon. *Viswaroopam*. 1.9 (1941): 288. Print.

Burton, Antoinette. "The Unfinished Business of Colonial Modernities." *Gender, Sexuality and Colonial Modernities*. Ed. Antoinette Burton. London: Routledge, 1999. 1-16. Print.

Bhattacharya, Tithi. "Tracking the Goddess: Religion, Community and Identity in the Durga Puja Ceremonies of Nineteenth Century Calcutta." *The Journal of Asian Studies* 66.4 (2007): 919-962. Print.

Cochin Saraswath Association. *A Request to Devadasi Communities*. Kochi: Cochin Saraswath Association, 1940. Print.

Cochin State: Secretary's Report. 20 Feb. 1941: *Huzur Secratariat Files*. Vol. 22. 1941.

Print.

Chatterjee, Partha. *The Nation and Its Fragments: Colonial and Postcolonial Histories*. New Delhi: Oxford UP, 1995. Print.

Dube, Saurabh. "Mapping Oppositions: Enchanted Spaces and Modern Places." *Unbecoming Modern: Colonialism, Modernity, Colonial Modernities.* Eds. Saurabh Dube and Ishita Bannerji-Dube. New Delhi: Social Science P, 2006. 76-94. Print.

Foucault, Michel. *The Archaeology of Knowledge*. Trans. A. M. Sheridan Smith. London, New York: Routledge, 2002. Print.

Hirsch, Marianne. *Family Frames: Photography, Narrative and Postmemory*. Cambridge: Harvard UP, 1997. Print.

Laxmi, Gangi. Petition to the Sarwadhikaryakkar. 29 Jan. 1942. C721/17*: Huzur Secratariat Files*. Govt. ofCochin. TS.

Letter from the Diwan's Office. 22 Nov. 1933. R2-11455/1108. *Huzur Secratariat Files.* Govt. of Cochin. TS.

Letter from S. Padmanabha. 26 Jan. 1942. B22. *Huzur Secratariat Files*. Govt of Cochin. TS.

Nair, K. Ramachandran, ed. *Gandhijiyum Keralavum*. 1979. Trivandrum: Dept. of Cultural Publications, Govt. of Kerala, 2003. Print.

Panikkar, Kavalam Narayana. "Devadasi System Unknown to Kerala." *Sahitya Nataka Academy Journal* 97.7-9 (1990): 56-62. Print.

Sanjayan. "Viswaveekshanam." *Viswaroopam*. 6.1 (1941): 173-76. Print.

Soman, P. *Devadasikalum Sahithya Charithravum*. Trivandrum: Prabath, 2000.
Print

2

Breaking Silence in Black and Dalit Women Autobiographies

— Reha Keer

What is silence? Silence is a part of communication. Silence is a part of paralanguage. It means that in this sense silence is a space provided to the listener so that he or she can understand or reflect over what is said. Silence of one give room to other one to speak up. Maintaining silence by will sometimes may be a healing therapy. It can also be a strategy to maintain distance. But forcing silence on someone is denying him/her speech. Thereby, denying expressing the self. When a powerful person imposes silence on the powerless, then silencing becomes a form of oppression. Thus, breaking silence can also be a means of healing and expressing the self. Breaking silence is a means to resist oppression. Breaking silence subverts power structures and converts rejection into resistance. It liberates. It gives a sense of freedom and empowerment. Roumen Dimitrov, in his essay "Explicit and Implicit Silence" writes, "silencing is bad while breaking silence is good."

Silence doesn't always mean consent. Silence is understanding present circumstances and reacting accordingly. It is possible that the 'weaker' one is not saying or reacting because he or she takes the full cognizance of the circumstances he or she caught in. "Silence is the ocean of the unsaid, the unspeakable, the repressed, the erased, the unheard". So what in this sense silence is? I mean, who are those who think their speech has no value? Or who are these who think their thoughts and assertion will go unheard? When silence is imposed it is intimidation and repression and hence, it has its psychological and political implications.

Women across nations, across societies and across patriarchies go unheard. They have always been denied speech. Rather, they have been made to think that their ideas or thoughts, moreover, their existence as human beings has no value. Their intellect has been suppressed by denying them speech. What gender stereotyping tells us that women are heart not mind; body, not head. Their beauty is adored and they have been hardly given chance to explore their intellectual abilities. From the very beginning of their lives they are told, sometimes implicitly and sometimes indirectly that they are not supposed to speak up. Thus, the present paper examines the silenced imposed on women (Dalit women and Afro-American women) marginalized within the community of women.

Blacks in America and Dalits in India have been silenced by rich whites and upper-caste-Hindus respectively. Within these specific marginalized groups black women and Dalit women stand out beyond the margins. Through the autobiographies of Black women, we come to know that it is not only race but gender also that make black women suffer more. Similarly, caste and gender intersectionality in the person of a Dalit woman become a source of subjugation and violence in multiple form. They have been doubly silenced.

But no matter how hard Dalit and black women's lot has been they fought against it. Writing down their lives or narrating it brought Dalit and Afro-American women into the fore and they broke silence through the autobiography. The autobiographies of blacks and Dalits reveal not only the ways through which they were silenced but negotiate or break silence strategically. Also, in doing so they leave an impact on the victimizer.

Thus, the present paper tries to study the strategies that the subaltern such as black women and Dalit women used to break silence by taking up Harriet Jacobs's autobiography *Incidents in the Life of a Slave Girl: An American Slave* (1861), Faustina Bama's *Karukku* (1992) and *Sangati* (1994). Black women autobiographers, whether it is Lucy Delaney or Harriet Jacobs bring to the fore that their gender has been the cause of their severe treatment in slavery. Dalit Feminists like Ruth Manorama, Urmila Pawar and Bama do talk about role of their gender when it comes to caste-based oppression. Thereby, both black women and Dalit women do break silence through their autobiographies.

The paper seeks to explore four questions: (1) what are the strategies adopted by victimizer to silent the victimized? (2) how the victimized negotiate the silence? (3) what impact does silencing make on the victimizer and the victim and vice-versa? Lastly, what are the categories of silence in the selected autobiographies?

Strategies to imposed silence:

Religion is followed unquestionably across societies. All 'norms' flow from religion. So, it is through religious scriptures and mythical stories that some people were silenced in the history of formation of slavery and caste. Haynes (2000) claims, that according to the Genesis 9 the Hamites were seen a cause of Noah's curse by blaming Hem and his descendants for 'foul' behaviour. Antebellum proslavery intellectuals in the defence of slavery exploited biblical myth of Noah's curse. Lee clarifies, "Though in the biblical account Noah and his family are not described in racial terms." It is through the gradual interpretations by Islamic, Christian and Jewish scholars that Hem came to be widely portrayed as black.

As far as Hindu religious texts such as the *Mahabharata* and the *Ramayana* are concerned, they preach that caste and caste system existed since the very times when gods were the inhabitants of earth. Therefore, caste is imbibed in the minds of the Hindus. In the *Mahabharata*, Karna, son of a charioteer, (though he is the first born of Kunti) is humiliated by Pandavas and Kripcharya in front of a crowd that assembled to watch Arjuna's and Karna's archery skills. Kripa addresses Karna, "It is only after knowing thy lineage that Partha can fight with thee, for high-born princes cannot engage in the single combat with unknown adventures" (Vyasa). Dronacharya does not teach archery to Eklavya, a tribal boy and when he hears that he has taught himself the skills of archery, he asks Eklavya to cut his thumb and give it to Drona as *gurudakshina*. In the *Ramayana*, Shabrai, a tribal woman offers weary Rama her hospitability. She serves him berries but only after testing them. Thus, she offers Rama *jootha*, (unclean) food, which he accepts and eats. It adds to the glory of Lord Rama. Since there are instances in scriptures themselves that gods belonged to one or the other caste, which was initially called *varna*, it is explicit that Hindus believed in caste and they act hardly debunk the rule of the caste. Consciously or unconsciously Hindus follow the patterns of caste and behave accordingly.

From religious texts comes the notion of purity and rules to be followed for maintaining it. For what such norms or rules serve to? The notion of purity and superiority of one caste or one race over the other caste or race a does not only contribute as social factor. It does have a materialistic base. Biblical myth was distorted in order to indoctrinate that blacks are inferior race, through which they could make them slaves and extracted maximum materialistic benefits from America. Why one set of people were called lower caste? Because they were needed to perform certain jobs. Precisely, menial jobs like manual scavenging.

In the case of black women, race and gender intersectionality is peculiar to their subjugation. While in the case of Dalit women, it is caste and gender that makes them stand out beyond the margins of caste-Hindu patriarchal society. For what purpose societies are patriarchal? Patriarchy is not only systematic exclusion of women from material benefits but by this systematic exclusion they are made dependent, meek, submissive and hence, silent.

Harriet Jacobs in her autobiography *Incidents in the Life of a Slave Girl (*1861) reveals a number of strategies that were used to silence blacks. Silencing their intellectual abilities is the very first tool through which they could control blacks. Harriet Jacobs writes, "Moreover, they thought he had spoiled his children, by teaching them to feel that they were human beings.

This was blasphemous doctrine for a slave to teach; presumptuous in him, and dangerous to the masters". Bama talks about constant insult and humiliations in school, "…every now and then, our class teacher, or the PT teacher would ask all the Harijan students to stand up, either at assembly, or during lessons…and if it happens to be a girl-child she is shut out away from studying."

Black women suffered inhuman sexual treatment at hands of their masters. They often faced sexual harassment and violent rapes. Hence, they became silent as they could not explicitly rebel against their master as they were afraid of getting killed by the master. Simultaneously, they could not tell their white mistress that they are the victim of her husband's inhuman treatment as it would enrage the mistress even more. "But I now entered on my fifteenth year--a sad epoch in the life of a slave girl. My master began to whisper foul words in my ear… I longed for someone to confide in. I would have given the world to have laid my head on my grandmother's faithful bosom, and told her all my troubles. But Dr. Flint swore he would kill me, if I was not as silent as the grave" (24). Thus, black women did not come to know at very early age that why they cannot confide in their mistress.

On the other, it is thought that Dalit women do have freedom as they can appear in the public sphere. It is here worth examining that why they were allowed to work outside. Dalit women were, due to their economic conditions, compelled to appear in the public sphere. The notion of 'pure' and 'impure' made Dalit women accessible to non-Dalit men. They undergo sexual harassment and subject to be raped violently.

In *Sangati*, Bama recalls that one day a young girl, Mariamma, from her community went to gather firewood in scorching sun and when she innocently went to drink some water from a nearby irrigation pump-set from the fields, which happened to be Kumaraswami Ayya's fields. Bama writes, "...he seized her hand and pulled her inside...When she came home and told her friends, they warned ger saying, "Mariamma, it is best if you shut up about this. If you even tell people what actually happened, you will find that it is you who will get the blame" (19-20).

Norman Coombs writes that slaves were inspected openly for any defect or disease. "The inspection was humiliating and degrading procedure. Men, women, and children usually appeared stark naked." Harriet Jacobs talks about the pain of mothers whose children were separated from them at a very tender age. No words could provide comfort to such mothers. They were rendered weak and helpless and thus silenced psychologically.

If silence on Dalits and blacks is imposed strategically then one has to counter that silence strategically. Bama, when receives praises of so many people when she was awarded a prize, she asks a question to herself, "Is it impossible for a Harijan to study or what?" and then she decides to prove that "we could study just as well as others" (21). It is through education that Bama gets materialistic comfort in her life. And the socio-political scenario of her life changes after acquiring education. Thus, she has been able to break socio-political silence imposed on her. Bama's grandmother and Jacobs grandmother earned some prestige in their respective communities.

Harriet Jacobs invents many tricks so that she could elude Dr. Flint and save herself from sexual harassment. Jacobs recalls, "By managing to keep within sight of people, as much as possible, during the day time, I had hitherto succeeded in eluding my master, though a razor was often held to my throat to force me to change this line of policy" (26).

Bama, in *Sangati,* challenges the internalized Brahmanical patriarchy within Dalit communities. She says it one justice for men and quite other for women. A woman, when gets irritated by men's constant insistence on Mariamma that she must beg pardon, says, "…none of them has the brains to find out whether it wasn't mudalaali who was doing wrong in the first place" (25).

The sense of collective identity is found both in Dalit women's autobiographies and black women autobiographies. In their narratives we do find an inherent essence of their respective cultures. They write their own life-stories by taking up pen in their own hands which marks their present in the dominant literary scenario.

The process of silencing does not only render the victim helpless and meek; it does affect the victimizer. As far as oppression of black women is concerned, both the white mistress and her white master shoe an enormous amount of wild and violent treatment. It makes both of them cruel, harsh, animalistic and inhuman. Instead of sympathizing with the black woman, the victim, the white mistress developed a hatred towards her. On the other hand, the forcefully silencing the victim psychologically depressed. They internalized the pattern of self- discrimination and slavery.

While countering silence strategically have filled Dalit and Black women with an enormous amount of self-confidence and made them able to assert their rights, it has certainly made the Hindu male caste oppressor and white male oppressor more enraged. The result of which has that they faced more violence.

There are several occasions when the victim intendedly remains silent. Jacobs in her narrative writes, "I have concealed the names of places, and given persons fictitious names. I had no motive for secrecy on my own account, but I deemed it kind and considerate towards others to pursue this course" (2). While, on the other hand, Bama remains silent unintendedly as she feels how to spoke up that the people involved in 'low-order jobs' in the same convent where she works as nun belong to her community.

Conclusion

There is scarcity of written accounts of the lives of Dalit and black women which reflects that women They were not given any chance to learn letters. Both, black women's autobiographies and Dalit women autobiographies formed a tradition within a tradition. Their narration of the self is a unique construction of their black woman and Dalit woman identity. They leave a legacy behind. By writing down their autobiographies both Dalit women and black women have broken the strictures of society. They ask several questions to their readers and engage them in their journey.

Works Cited

Ambedkar, B.R. *The Untouchables: Who were they and why they became Untouchables.* Kalpaz Publications. Reprint 2017

Bama, Faustina. Karukku. Trans. From Tamil by Lakshmi Holmstrom, Oxford India Paperback, 2018.

Bama, Faustina. Sangati. Trans. From Tamil by Lakshmi Holmstrom. Oxford University Press, 2006.

Coombs, Norman. *Black Experience in America.* Start Classics, 2013.

Deliege, Robert. *The Untouchables of India.* Translated from French By Nora Scoot, Berg, 1999.

Dimitrov, Roumen. "Explicit and Implicit Silence." *Journal of Advertising and Public Relations.* Shyahwa Publications, Vol. 2, Issue 1, 2019, pp 19-31. http://www.sryahwapublications.com. Accessed 26 April 2019.

Haynes, Stephen R. "Original Dishonor: Naoh's Curse and the Southern Defense of Slavery." *Journal of Southern Relgion.* 2000. http://www.jsr.fsu.edu/honor.htm. Accessed 08 May 2019.

Jacobs, Harriet. *Incidents in the Life of a Slave Girl.* Leonaou Ltd., 2011.

Lee, Felicia R. "From Noah's Curse to Slavery's Rationale." *The New York Times.* http://www.nytimes.com. Accessed 11 May 2019.

M. Braxton, Joanne. *The Cambridge Companion To African American Women's Literature.* Cambridge University Press, 2010.

M. Stover, Johnnie. *Rhetoric and Resistance in Black Women's Autobiography.* University Press of Florida, 2003.

3

Caste and Class Struggle: Studying the Marginalization of Potters of India

— *Sangeeta Jawla*

This paper will examine the Indian pottery making tradition and the narratives that have emerged from it. This art of pottery making, according to the Varna system is traditionally associated with the caste of the kumhars in north India. These narratives are about the pot, potters and pottery, and touch upon issue like myths of origin, life narratives, migration tales as well as their class and caste struggles. The paper is based on the three levels of narratives- 1. The real life narratives of the contemporary potters residing in various parts of India; 2. The folklore which is preserved with the potters and is collected from various parts in India; 3. The narratives written by Indian authors on pot, potter or pottery.

Krishnan's book on pottery begins with the following epigraph from Fitzgerald's Rubaiyat of Omar Khayyam "All this of pot and potter- Tell me, Then, who makes- who sells- who buys- who is the pot?" (5).

Pottery is the most intense among other arts. The pot creates relations- 'relations between nature and culture, between individual and society, between utility and beauty.' (Glassie 27) The contemporary social location and social structure of the potters' community in Rajasthan and Haryana is explicated here. When we look at the contemporary potters of north India they seem to face many problems such as caste related issues- for instance, the potters of Haryana themselves say that they don't have unity among themselves and therefore whenever they want to put their issues in front of the village bodies, they fail. Potters need ample space for kiln and for keeping the pots for drying, but there seems to be a dearth of land for the poor potter families. In the villages that I visited, clay and fuel are getting costlier. Clay used to come from the nearby water resources but is now procured seasonally from far-off villages.

The villages that I visited were part of Haryana, a northern state of India. I chose six villages- Nidana, Chabri, Dhigana, Bharon Khera, Lalit Khera, Nizampur from Jind (an administrative division) along with Shehri, Khanda and Cholka from Kharkhoda (a city in Sonipat district of Haryana). Along with these, the major parts of my field work were Alwar and Jodhpur in Rajasthan and a small town Uttam Nagar, where potters have shifted either from the villages of Haryana or from Alwar. The younger generations want to get educated for better jobs. A decline in the domestic demand for pottery has caused a further setback. Modern appliances like refrigerators have replaced earthen ware meant to store water and other items. And even the potter's wheel is run by electricity. One villager said, *Isi dhandhe mai lge rhe to hmaari jaati aage nahi badh sakti* (If we continue this occupation, our caste would not be able to flourish). Those who continue to be potters don't know how to expand their business as they've never travelled to places outside their villages and have less of exposure. Though not everybody is keen upon giving up this tradition as one of them says that *Aaj bhi hmaare ghro mai ye kiya jaata hai taaki parampara aage badhti rhe* (We still practice this art form even today so that our tradition retains.) They make *matkaa* (pitchers), *kaapan* (lids), *diya* (oil lamps), *kulhad* (for serving), *shakora, baloni* (goblets), *surahi, karva* and *lota* (tumblers). They are paid in cash or kind. The practice of bartering wheat/grains for the clay vessels can still be seen. Vimla from Nidana village says *Kaam acha hai par daam acha nahi hai* (This work is good but the pay is not good). The designs as well as the paint and brushes are made of natural material. As the process is deeply organic, the vessels do not have the metallic finish of similar items sold in cities during festivals and other occasions. Instead, they use *gerua* (orange colour) with black and white patterns, including motifs like snakes and birds.

Potters try to understand their roots, personal histories, community histories through pots. They sculpt not just pottery but their present and future through it. And the pot allows them to give a shape to the lives as pot is itself given shape by the potters. The real life artefacts that are created by the potter and with that, happens a creation of the narratives that surrounds this material. There are variety of stories that revolve around the art of pottery making and pottery as a metaphor is used by different authors to resolve the real life issues such as Vijaydan Detha's "Ghade ki Seekh" (Lesson of a Pot). In this story, pot, a non- living material talks to a farmer who goes to commit suicide and tells him that the pot has many more problems than the farmers has in his life and in the end saves the farmer's life. This story doesn't just focus on the problem of the farmer or a pot but it also tells us the tragic life that a potter also goes through. When we look at some of the instances from this short story, we get to know that there are certain deep ideas that are associated within. For instance the pot says at one point- "Pagle, ghade jitna gyaan to rishi-muniyo mai bhi nahi hota." ("Oh fool! Even the sages don't have the knowledge that a pot has"). In the stories of potters, they always have something to say about the caste issues. They always show in their stories that the potter caste is better in all ways than the Brahmin, the priestly caste. Kumhars place themselves at par with Brahmins as they say they've emerged from Brahma. Brahma, the Hindu God once gave a piece of sugarcane to 36 communities but it's only the potter who kept the piece alive as it grows near his clay and therefore Kumhar is given blessings by the god. Even the god Prahalad (a devotee ruler mentioned in Purana) become the devotee of a potter spouse who help him saving a kitten who got stuck in a pot which was kept in the kiln. One can observe that how such small communities and tribes of India utilize the language and religion to express their identity. It is said that the potters and brahmins have always been part of the vedic rituals because brahmins have knowledge but they lack the skills that a potter has- "Even though the artisan is not directly mentioned therein, it has to be presumed that the artisan was necessary even according to the older scriptures, because the priest, who is the chief executive in any sacrifice, is hardly expected to carry out the skilled job" (Kashikar 19).

There are two folk tales which are part of the collections by A.K. Ramanujan such as "The Clay Mother-in-Law" and "Gandharva Sen is Dead." The first story tells us that how a potter can give any shape to the clay he touches. In this particular story, he gives the clay shape of a human being that seems alive to the ones who loved her. This clay mother-in-law is loved by the daughter-in-law but is used for benefits by the son and the neighbours. And the story has a tragic end where the clay mother-in-law is broken into pieces and nobody gained anything from this material being. The latter story is that of a donkey that holds importance in a potter's life in real. The king in the story gets to know that Gandharva Sen dies and starts crying. Along with the king, the other people of his kingdom also cried but when they all got to know that Gandharva Sen was nobody but a potter's donkey, they all started laughing. The tragedy in this story, which is seen as a quip among the other funny folktales, is that the potter was crying in reality on the tragic death of his donkey which he used to gather clay from faraway places. There is other very interesting element connected to the story- AK Ramanujan collected this tale from Bengal and when I did my field research among the potters of north India, I found this same story with the contemporary potters though the telling was different. Therefore, one can say that this is how the folklore in general and folktales in particular travel from one place to another. The other interesting story on donkey tells why a potter has a donkey but any other animal as his pet. Once upon a time, a potter goes to the god and asks for an animal which can carry clay for him and can be easily fed by a poor potter. God gives him an elephant but the potter wasn't happy and said if he could get an animal which can easily fit in his small house. God gives him a camel but the camel had humps on which the clay can't be easily carried. In the end god gives him a donkey which can feed itself and can carry clay easily. The plasticity of clay keeps the object alive and hence brings plasticity to the narratives too. There is a story at the end of Ramanujan's essay "When Mirrors Are Windows" and the story takes us to a realm where we can see various magical qualities attached to a pot. A pot is found by a spouse called Kallu and Raziya who gets to know that this pot can double anything that falls into it. Both of them used the pot to increase their wealth just like the clay mother-in-law was used by the son. There are various such magical myths that are found associated with a pot. A pot has always something to say in different narratives. There are various other ways in which a 'pot' is used as a metaphor. For instance the Urdu poets have used it in many ways. One such example is-

Abhi to chaak pe jaari hai raksh mitti ka
Abhi kumhar ki niyat badal bhi sakti hai

("The dance of the clay is still happening onto the potter's wheel. The intent of the potter can still change its shape"). This particular *sher*/couplet brings a live movement in the clay. The clay is seen as a dancing body which the potter sees as a woman. There could be many interpretations to this particular couplet. The potter as a creator falls in love with his creation therefore the idea of incest can be related. Touching the potter wheel in north India is seen as a prerogative of the male potters and women are not allowed to touch the wheel and give shape to the clay because they are seen as impure beings and the skill is always associated with the male potters only. Also, the shape of the clay on the wheel is seen as similar to phallus and therefore if the clay is dancing and the male potter is attracted towards it one can bring the element of homosexuality as well.

Along with Urdu Shayeri, the importance of pot and potters can be seen in an oral epic which is sung by the Nath community of Rajasthan called 'The Carnival of Parting." In this epic there is a small incident when the donkey, Gandharva Sen starts speaking to his potter owner at night and demands him to let the king's daughter marry him. The potter gets scared and wants to take his family and the donkey away from this kingdom but all the villagers stop the potter because in those times, a potter and his pottery had much importance. The potters used to provide the common household utensils and even the marriage and festival rituals were incomplete without potter's utensils and wheel. When the villagers get to know the reason of potter's departure, they also get scared and want to leave the village altogether but the king stops all the villagers and agrees to marry his daughter to Gandharva Sen. With this story one can make connections to the migration of potters that happens in today's times. In this story the villagers didn't allow the potter's family to leave the village because of their importance for the villagers, though in contemporary times, the kumhars hold no value for the villagers of either Haryana or Rajasthan because one can easily get the pottery at their homes in very less price and time. Therefore, the migration of potters and similar other artisans is quite common today.

There are many time periods covered through these narratives. The day to day problems are depicted through them and one can look for the solutions and if not that, then at least compare it to the real life issues the potters face today. Few stories such as the story of a saint called Sant Gora Kumbhar is prominent to understand the Bhakti movement in India. The story revolves around a kumbhar/potter who pray his god while kneading the clay and he was so devoted into this worship that he crushes his only child with the clay. After this incident the life of the kumbhar spouse goes through turbulence but all this is solved only by praying the god again. This story is part of the children's handbooks and there are five movies available in five different languages that are based on this story.

One can see the amalgamations among the tales collected from the contemporary potters, and the tales that revolve around pot, potter and pottery as metaphors, taken by the Indian authors for study. It can be therefore said that 'pot' is not just useful for the archaeological study but can be read under the purview of folklore and Literature where narratives around pottery can be seen as having importance in the lives of the potters of contemporary India.

Works Cited

Bhakata Gora Kumbhar. Dir. ArvindTrivedi.Goldmine Gujarati Movies, 1978. Film.

Campkin, Ben. (2013). "Placing "Matter Out of Place": Purity and Danger as Evidence for Architecture and Urbanism."

Casey, Edward S. (1996) "How to Get from Space to Place in a Fairly Short Stress."

Detha, Vijaydan. *The Dilemma and Other Stories*. New Delhi: ManushiPrakashan, 1997. Print.

Dharwadker, Vinay. (1999). *The Collected Essays of A.K. Ramanujan*. New Delhi: Oxford University Press.

Dyk, Walter. Son of Old Man Hat. Lincoln: University of Nebraska Press, 1967. Print.

Glassie, Henry. *The Potters' Art*. Bloomington: Indiana University Press. Print. 1999.

Gold, Ann Grodzins, eds. *A Carnival of Parting: The Tales of King Bharthari and King Gopi Chand as Sung and Told by MadhuNatisarNath of Ghatiyali*, Rajasthan. New Delhi: MunshiramManoharlal Publishers, 1993. Print.

Hemion, Timothy. *Inspector Morimoto and the Famous Potter: A Detective Story Set in Japan*. USA: iUniverse. Print. 2004.

Hill, Laban Carrick. Illustrated by Bryan Collier.*Dave the Potter: Artist, Poet, Slave.*Little, Brown Books for Young Readers Print. 2010.

Hillerman, Tony. *A Thief of Time*. New York: Harper Collins Publishers. Print. 2009.

Isik, Damla. (2010)."Personal and Global Economics: Male Carpet Manufacturers as Entrepreneurs in the Weaving Neighborhoods of Konya, Turkey."

Jayakar, Pupul. *Invisible Order, Tribute to Haku Shah*. New Delhi: Art Indus, 1999. Print.

Kashikar, C.G. (1969). "Pottery in the Vedic Literature."

Krishnan, Shantha. *Traditional Potters: Entitlements and Enablements of Artisans.* New Delhi: Indus Publ. Co., 1989. Print.

Kroeber, Theodora. Ishi in Two Worlds: A Biography of the Last Wild Indian in North America. London: University of California Press, 1973. Print.

Liebl, Maureen & Tirthankar Roy. (2003) "Handmade in India: Preliminary Analysis of Crafts Producers and Crafts Production."

Liebl, Maureen &Tirthankar Roy. "Handmade in India: Preliminary Analysis of Crafts Producers and Crafts Production."

Lucas, Gavin. (2003) "Reading Pottery: Literature and Transfer- Printed Pottery in the Early Nineteenth Century."

Propp, Vladimir. Morphology of Folktales. Austin: University of Texas Press, 1968. Print.

*The Collected Essays of A.K. Ramanujan.*Ed. Dharwadker, Vinay. New Delhi: Oxford University Press, 1999. Print.

Trivedi, Arvind, &Raval, Dinesh. (1978). *Bhagat Gora Kumbhar.* India: Goldmine Gujarati Movies.

4

Ethnic Conflict in *Funny Boy*

— ***Santu Neog***

Funny Boy by Shyam Selvadurai is an acute portrayal of ethnic violence between two ethnic groups – the Sinhalese and the Tamils in postcolonial Sri Lanka. Sri Lanka witnessed one of the most brutal civil wars after its independence in 1948 that led to a large scale displacement. In this paper I will show the ways Shyam Selvadurai depicts ethnic riots, the crisis of the nation state and nationalism in postcolonial Sri Lanka and the text giving voice to the silent aspects of conflict, especially the human condition by exploring the subjectivities rooted in history. In his "Introduction" to *Sri Lanka: History and the roots of conflict*, Jonathan Spencer writes:

> In 1948 the colony of Ceylon was granted independence by Britain. Forty years later the island (renamed Sri Lanka in 1972) lurches from political crisis to political crisis. Large sections of its territory in the north and the east have been under de facto control of troops of the Indian Peace Keeping Force (IPKF), although that control was still regularly threatened by the activities of various militant Tamil separatist groups. (1)

The crisis between the two communities, the Sinhalese and the Tamils, I argue, was primarily because of the idea of nationalism as Selvadurai would show us. In the essay,"Newspaper nationalism: Sinhala identity as historical discourse," Serena Tennekoon writes:

> National identity is most vigorously affirmed when it becomes most problematic. In Sri Lanka, the dramatic escalation of ethnic conflict between the Sinhala majority and the Tamil minority, especially during the last few years, has generated a national identity crisis. (205)

Nationalism as a concept was problematic since it demands a homogeneity which was witnessed in Sri Lanka. In the novel *Funny Boy* Selvadurai depicts this crisis through the protagonist Arjie.

In the novel Arjie was offered to be admitted on a Sinhalese language school since Sinhalese was seen as "the real language of the future." I argue that Selvadurai shows the crisis of nationalism here, where the dominant language is installed as the national language and the minority cultures are subverted. In fact in the year 1956, the government of S. W. R. D. Bandarnaike installed Sinhalese as the national language of Sri Lanka. Hence it is evident here that Selvadurai sharply points to the relation between language and nationalism through Arjie. It is once again shown in the text where Appa, Arjie's father points out the severe crisis that Sinhalese nationalism has brought in:

> The Sinhalese wanted to make Sinhala the only national language, and the Tamils did not like this. So there was a riot and many Tamils were killed. (*Funny Boy*, 60)

Therefore the text, I argue, shows the reason behind the strife that it was primarily nationalism which was the root of the conflict. Ashis Nandy points out in this insecurity of nationalism in his essay,"Nationalism, Genuine and Spurious":

> Nationalism insists on the primacy of national identity over identities built on subnational allegiances—religions, castes, sects, linguistic affiliations, and ethnicities. It promotes

> decontextualized formulas or slogans like 'We are Indians first, then Hindus, Tamils, or Dalits,' for nationalism expects all identities to be subservient to the interests of the national state. As a general rule, nationalism fears other identities as potential rivals and subversive presences. (7)

Similarly I argue that *Funny Boy* brings out this crisis by showing ethnic tensions in the form of riots and violence. Since Sinhalese identity was given preference the Tamil community and its identity was subverted. As Nandy said, it could be seen that Sinhalese nationalism feared the presence of other cultures and infact looked at the Tamil community as its rivals for which it tried to impose a Sinhalese identity on the Tamils. Selvadurai depicts the gradual transition of Sri Lankan society within modernity where the Tamil community was gradually adapting itself to nationalism and its homogenous tendency. In the Chapter, "Small Choices" he depicts the different ways the Tamil community adjusts itself. For instance, when a Sinhalese man tried to paste a poster with the lamp on the wall to which Jegan, son of a friend of Arjie's father, reacted. Selvadurai depicts this in the book:

> 'This is a private wall,' Jegan said. 'If you don't stop that now, we're going to call the police.'
>
> The man smiled at Jegan and smiled at him to do so. (*Funny Boy*, 168)

I argue that this instance describes the way the dominant community was asserting itself on the Tamil community where people did not even fear the law and infact the smile is suggestive of the police being biased. Moreover this incident continues till Jegan fights the person and he shouts, 'You don't know who you are dealing with' (*Funny Boy*, 168). Selvadurai brings out a hostile approach where the Tamil community was subjugated totally and questioning the law itself. It is noticeable to look at the reply of Appa to this incident:

> My father turned to Jegan. 'You shouldn't have done that.'

> Jegan looked at him in surprise. 'Why uncle?' he said. He sounded hurt.
>
> 'These days it is necessary to be discreet. We could have let him put up the poster and torn it down later.' (*Funny Boy*, 169)

Appa's reply shows the fear amidst the Tamil community. Hence Appa is making small choices of adjusting to this new crisis. Appa further says when Jegan replies back as the act being illegal: 'That's not the point' my father said. 'One must be careful not to antagonize the wrong people.' (*Funny Boy*,169).

Despite knowing that the act was illegal, still making a compromise was a traumatic situation that Selvadurai shows. These small choices are made for survival. The angst and the fear are brought out again when their neighbour said,

> 'It seems that they are doing this everywhere,' Mrs. Bandara, the neighbor who lived across the road from us, said. 'They put a lamp banner in some woman's garden and when she protested they assaulted her.' (*Funny Boy*, 169)

This again showed the crisis of the Tamil community under an aggressive nationalism which tortures people co-existing in the same place for centuries. This is the problem of nationalism within the formation of the nation-state where the concept of nationalism is linked to postcolonial state formation. Ashis Nandy writes in his book, *The Romance of the State: And the Fate of Dissent in the Tropics*: 'From the very beginning, nation-building – a polite term for the cultural and ideological homogenization of a country's population – became one of stated or implicit goals of the modern state" (2). Hence, I argue that Selvadurai is pointing out to a crisis which has a broader structure. This structure can be seen connected with modernity since the ideas of nation-state and nationalism were connected. It is worth citing Ashis Nandy here where he writes on nationalism that 'the concept would never have attained the power it later did if the French Revolution had not underwritten it by linking the state, or statehood, with nationalism' (*The Romance of the State*, 2). I argue that Selvadurai throws an important perspective through the depiction of ethnic strife. The idea of modernity and state formation in postcolonial societies and the link with nationalism and a national language are brilliantly portrayed when he shows the two communities engaging in violence. It also questions the redeeming role of history that comes with the Enlightenment where modernity turned destructive wiping out identities. Hence history in the text is shown as traumatic and full of conflicts and non redeeming. Nationalism is shown as divisive rather than inclusive where it splits communities hitherto living harmoniously. The demand of the Tamil community for a different state is also depicted where Tamil people took to arms. Selvadurai writes:

> There was a group in Jaffna called the Tamil Tigers. They wanted a separate country and the Sinhalese were very angry about this. Ammachi often talked about the Tigers. She was on their side and declared that if they did get a separate state, which they would call Elam, she would be the first to go and stay there. (*Funny Boy*, 61)

It is necessary to mention about the Liberation Tigers of Tamil Elam here which Selvadurai mentions as Tigers. Selvadurai poignantly brings forth this issue and shows the trauma of nationalism where people are forced to take up arms to defend their identities. Hence I argue, Selvadurai looks at a broader picture trying to explore the structural problems involved within the nation-state where plurality of cultures are not accepted. A community which was living in their homeland was now gradually becoming homeless. This sense of homelessness was the reason for the armed rebellion that Selvadurai mentions above. Infact, the novel portrays the ethnic tensions very sharply. The last chapter of the novel is named "Riot Journal: An Epilogue" which portrays the violence carried out. The description of riots is painful. Selvadurai writes:

> Appa was on the phone and, from the expression of his face, we knew that something had happened. Finally he put the phone

> down. 'That was Mala,' he said. Then he told us that there was trouble in Colombo. All the Tamil houses near the Kanaththa Cemetery had been burnt. We stared at him, unable to believe what he was saying. (*Funny Boy*, 286)

The depiction of riots that all the houses were burnt down is significant and shows the ethnic conflict in the height of its violence. Further when Amma, Arjie's mother asked about the reason about the burning down of houses, Appa explained that it was because of the killings of the Tigers. Selvadurai writes:

> Appa explained that it was because of the thirteen soldiers who were killed by the Tigers two days ago. The funeral was held last night and the mob at the cemetery went on a rampage. (*Funny Boy*, 286)

It is clearly seen that both the parties, the government and the Tamil tigers are now involved in mutual hostility towards each other. The important part is that people killed civilians. The entire Tamil population was seen as enemy fighting against the Sinhalese population. This situation between the two communities brings out the individual and collective trauma and loss of lives during the civil war. It is again heightened when this trauma is tried to be ignored and normalized. Selvadurai points this out when he shows Appa denying this riot. He writes, 'Appa tried to dismiss the whole thing. He told us to go to bed, that it was only a rumour, that there was probably some gang fight in a slum around Kanaththa which people were calling a communal riot. But I haven't been able to sleep. I have tried to read, but that is impossible, too. The only thing for me to do is write' (*Funny Boy*, 286-287).

The denial of the conflict portrays the fear that these people are undergoing. The constant denial also becomes a source of survival. Selvadurai brings out the silences hidden inside the characters. He portrays the agony that Arjie is going through being unable to sleep and let out his suffering for which he finally writes to assuage the pain. The novel depicts the gradual loss of faith in the government as well when people thought about the involvement of the government in the riot. Arjie's mother is talking to Sena uncle and Chithra aunty, when Arjie overhears the discussion:

> 'How can the government be doing this?' Amma was saying bitterly. 'After all, we Tamils helped vote them in.'
> 'We're not one hundred percent sure that they are behind the rioting,' my father said.
> 'Of course they are. If not, why aren't they declaring curfew, and why aren't the police and army stopping the mobs?' (*Funny Boy*, 289)

This discussion brings out the way people are looking at the government which once they voted for but who has been working only for a particular community. Hence ethnic conflict here also creates doubts in the involvement of state power in order to legitimize a dominant national identity. The depiction of the riots and violence is present throughout the chapter. Another instance is that of a family burnt inside the car. Selvadurai writes, 'The family in the car were simply staring out at the thugs as if they didn't realize what was going on. Now one of the thugs began to ask around for a match' (*Funny Boy*, 292). Selvadurai acutely describes these incidents where people were massacred as a result of the ethnic strife, the extent of violence when people fail to empathize with other people and start looking at them as enemies. I argue that all these incidents are connected to the crisis of nationalism. Benedict Anderson writes in his book, *Imagined Community* on this emptiness of the concept of nationalism, 'Firstly it is imagined as a community, because, regardless of the actual inequality and exploitation that may prevail in each, the nation is always conceived as a deep, horizontal comradeship' (7). I argue that Selvadurai brings out this crisis where the exploitation of the Tamil community is neither felt nor seen. The actual inequality and exploitation are hidden where people were killed, displaced and wiped out of their identities in their homeland. Instead the nation still exists as Anderson says in an imagined comradeship where people imagines of an underlying deep unity. This divisiveness and blindness is something, I argue, that Selvadurai portrays. Further it is important to see how people were living in trauma prepared for riots to happen anytime by describing how Amma and Appa asked Arjie to be ready. He writes:

> She explained to us that we have to be prepared if the mob comes. She and Appa have worked out an escape plan. She asked us to follow her onto the back verandah. In the back garden I saw that our ladder has been placed against the side wall. If the mob comes, we are to climb up the ladder and jump over the wall into the Perera's back garden. Perera aunty and Perera uncle will hide us in their storeroom. (*Funny Boy*, 293)

Selvadurai is bringing out not only the traumatic subjectivities of certain individuals here, but symbolically of the entire Tamil population. He is bringing out the human condition of people during ethnic conflicts and looks at the subjectivities rooted in history. I argue that Selvadurai brings these instances to unravel the anxieties and understand history not only as facts but to understand it through human subjectivities such that lives of people are empathized and the entire situation becomes clear.

Finally, the novel depicts the migration to Canada where communities living in their homeland have to flee or are exiled because Sri Lanka as a nation-state burdened with nationalism failed to accommodate diversity. Selvadurai writes,'Today I received my passport. As I looked at it, I finally realized that we were really leaving Sri Lanka; that in two days we will be in a strange country' (*Funny Boy*, 308). It is clear from the word "strange" about the uncertainties, the fears and anxieties of leaving one's homeland. Selvadurai brings out this idea of a loss of home, the trauma of being exiled into something strange and the feeling of exile. He further writes, 'I don't think that we ever imagined we would go abroad under these circumstances, as penniless refugees. We are going, not with the idea that something delightful awaits us, but rather with the knowledge that great difficulties lie ahead' (*Funny Boy*, 308). Hence the ethnic conflict not only stripped off the identity of the Tamil population, but it was devastating where it displaced people, killed people and made them foreigners in their own territory. I would finally say that Selvadurai portrays the ethnic conflict poignantly looking at the structures of the conflict from nationalism to nation-state bringing out unnoticed and silent aspects of history and the crisis people went through as a consequence of it.

Works Cited

Anderson, Benedict. *Imagined Communities: Reflections on the Origin and Spread of Nationalism*. 1983. New ed. London: Verso, 2006. Print.

Nandy, Ashis. *The Romance of the State: And the Fate of Dissent in the Tropics*. New Delhi: Oxford UP, 2003. Print.

---. "Nationalism, Genuine and Spurious: A very late obituary of two early post-nationalist strains in India." Web. 10 Jan. 2016.

Selvadurai, Shyam. *Funny Boy*. Gurgaon: Penguin Random House India, 1994. Print.

Spencer, Jonathan. "Introduction: the power of the past." *Sri Lanka: History and the Roots of Conflict*. Ed. Jonathan Spencer. 1990. London: Routledge,2004. 1-16. Print.

Tennekoon, Serena. "Newspaper nationalism: Sinhala identity as historical discourse." *SriLanka: History and the roots of conflict*. Ed. Jonathan Spencer. 1990. London:Routledge, 2004. 205-226. Print.

5

Dalit Feminists as Public Intellectuals: A Study of Resistance to Patriarchal Discourse in the Works of Bama and Meena Kandasamy

— *Swasti Sharma*

Intellectuals are critical thinkers who meditate on the conflicts within the society to which they belong .They often propose solutions for such normative problems and subsequently acquire the status of a public representatives .They either affirm or contest the dominant discourse either by dismissing, generating or endorsing an ideology, or by defending a particular set of values. One of the most coherent articulations of intellectuals can be drawn from Gramsci's *Prison Notebooks* , in which he has compared and contrasted 'organic' and 'traditional' intellectuals. It is the organic intellectuals who, through their organizational skills, displace the traditional intelligentsia. According to Gramsci ,

> Every social group, coming into existence on the original terrain of an essential function in the world of economic production, creates together with itself, organically, one or more strata of intellectuals which give it homogeneity and an awareness of its

> own function not only in the economic but also in the social and political fields.(Gramsci 29)

The organic intellectuals assume leadership roles and perform directive functions. It is imperative to comprehend the difference between an academic and a public intellectual. While academics operate within the institutional framework, public intellectuals transcend these boundaries through theorisation. They indulge in social activism and communicate interests of the lowest rung on the ladder. Nevertheless, public intellectuals are not exempted from ideological subjectivity.They too operate in the marketplace of ideas. At the third Nikhil Chakravartty Memorial Lecture delivered on 26 October 2014, Romila Thapar reiterated the role and responsibility of public intellectuals in India. She identified Jyotiba Phule as the foremost dissenting voice. Phule regarded Aryan invasion as the onset of systematic oppression of indigenous inhabitants i.e. the Dalits. Romila Thapar has underlined the differences between an academic and a public intellectual through the examples of Phule and Periyar. While academics are characterised by complacent attitude towards the perils of democracy, public intellectuals seek resolution. She has placed premium on the autonomy of public intellectuals to differentiate between right and wrong. This notion shall remain a frame of reference during the course of this research paper.

The social equations of caste and gender are determined by exercise of power in the form of hegemony. The term 'hegemony' in the feminist context is used as shorthand to delineate the relatively dominant stature of a patriarchal ideas and their associated inclination to become commonsensical and intuitive, thereby inhibiting the dissemination or even the existence of alternative ideas. In *The Second Sex,* French existentialist Simone de Beauvoir aptly noted, "Representation of the world, like the world itself, is the work of men; they describe it from their own point of view, which they confuse with absolute truth."(Beauvoir, 152) American philosopher and gender theorist Judith Butler has remarked that Beauvoir's observation, "One is not born, but rather becomes, a woman" differentiates between "sex" and "gender". Sex is a biological identity while gender is a social construct. According to Butler, gender is "a stylized repetition of acts...which are internally discontinuous...[so that] the appearance of substance is precisely that, a constructed identity, a performative accomplishment which the mundane social audience, including the actors themselves, come to believe and to perform in the mode of belief (Butler, 519)." By imitating the conventions, gender becomes commodified and subservience is accomplished. A feminist discourse is located at the intersection of class ,ethnicity and sexuality. Butler and many third-wave feminists have made attempts to redefine feminism in order to ensure that any gendered pronoun is eliminated. The binary of subject/object constitutes the basic assumption for feminist practices. The preliminary function of a feminist is to expose any hegemonic or artificial division imposed on women. Parody is an instrument through which the undertone of gender bias is unmasked. Since time immemorial ,the roles deemed appropriate for men (to be considered masculine) and women (to be considered feminine) have been transmitted from one generation to another to produce a social environment that both sustains and legitimizes a seemingly natural gender binary. The dominant discourse does not recognise fluidity of gender. Therefore ,challenging reproductive heteronormativity is also a crucial project undertaken by many feminists across the globe.

Dalit women are subjected to triple marginalization in India. Their existence is governed by the factors of caste, class and gender. They are coerced to uphold middle-class gendered norms of sexuality and marriage, which propagate patriarchal notions of domesticity and service, while simultaneously being prone to violence. Till the first half of the twentieth century, there was no uniform or solidified dalit feminist movement in India. It was during the 1990s that the formation of autonomous dalit women's organisations turned the identity politics upside down.With the establishment of National Federation of Dalit Women and the All India Dalit Women's Forum, Dalit feminists began vehemently resisting the collective and public threat of rape, sexual assault and physical violence at the work place and in domestic sphere. In Sharmila Rege's words "The assertion of autonomous dalit women's organisations in the 1990s threw up several crucial theoretical and political challenges, besides underlining the brahmanism of the feminist movement and the patriarchal practices of dalit politics." (Rege, WS-39)

The decade witnessed a surge of caste consciousness and revolutionary potential. It was for the very first time that homogenization of dalit women's lived experiences was challenged. In post-independent India ,male dalit writers were accommodating strong women characters in their literary corpus but they were unable to empathise adequately. For instance, Sharankumar Limable's magnum opus *Akkarmashi* (1984) highlighted the struggle of Masamai. It explored the plight of a dalit woman who was sexually abused, raped and tormented by the upper-caste Hanmanta Limbale. Yet, the powerlessness endured by an underprivileged single mother is underrepresented. In addition, the hostile treatment inflicted by the members of her own caste and the constant anxiety of being sexually vulnerable are major issues which remain suppressed.

One must acknowledge that social rank held by an individual determines the perception of reality and therefore non-dalit women's portrayal of the woes of dalit women may be categorised as sympathetic but it is not authentic. Since 1970s, the feminist theorisation has seen decline in its dependence on left politics. Many feminists had argued that marxist model of base and superstructure could not capture the intricacies of feminist epistemology. Two major overlapping positions have emerged from the struggles and politics of dalit women. The earliest is the Marxist/ Phule-Ambedkarite position of the Satyashodak Mahila Sabha. Another one which originates from the dalit- bahujan alliance is known as the Bahujan Mahila Mahasangh (BMM) which aims at the revival of Bahujan tradition. The risk of glorifying Bahujan community and cultural practices involves the risk of vindicating patriarchal power within the dalit community.The Dalit Mahila Sanghatana has been extremely critical of the continuation of Manu's influence even among the dalit male who otherwise traces his lineage to a Phule Ambedkarite ideology (Rege, WS-40).

The literature of dalit women largely deals with issues of violence and oppression based on their everyday experience .Most importantly, it exposes the spiral of silence which prevents dalit women from stating their opinions. The fear of social exclusion hinders their psychological advancement and decision-making capacity.They surrender to the dominant ideologies consequently. The humiliation of being the target of abuse promotes self-loathing and diminishes self-worth exponentially. Dalit women's bodies, sexuality, and reproductive preferences are directly related to the cultural hegemony of the caste-gender status quo in India, with chastity and endogamy playing crucial role in maintaining caste boundaries. In dalit women's writings, multiple, intertwined identities as women, workers, and dalits are negotiated through pluralistic discourse. Dalit feminist writers like Bama and Meena Kandasamy have constructed a sense of selfhood through their writings. They have examined the dilemmas about matrimonial choices and domestic violence. They have outlined the process which facilitates a transparent understanding of agency and gender relations, as dynamic, fluid, and converging in response to changing experiences and subjectivities.

Bama Faustina Soosairaj is a Tamil Dalit feminist. Her autobiographical narrative *Karukku* (1992) has put her on the literary map. The story explicates the joys and sorrows as encountered by Dalit Christian women in Tamil Nadu. She has authored nearly twenty short stories.Bama served as a nun for seven years and then left the church to focus on writing. She has recounted events from her childhood that left indelible impression on her mind. After the publication of her narrative, she was banished from her village for several months. She has managed to successfully set up a school for Dalit children in Uttiramerur. Her works embody core dalit feminist values and manifest inner strength of subaltern women.

In her autobiography, she raised a pertinent question: "Are Dalits not human beings? Do they not have common sense? Do they not have such attributes as a sense of honour and self-respect? Are they without any wisdom, beauty, dignity? What do we lack?" (Bama, 27). On completing her graduation, Bama chose to become a schoolteacher for underclass girls. According to her, religious conversion was a medium to escape caste-based discrimination and to foster her agenda of catering to the needs of poor dalit girls.However, she soon discovered rampant prejudice within ecclesiastical society. Enraged by the facade of egalitarianism, she left the church and pursued academic venture .Bama has exposed oppression of dalit children and scholars by Catholic nuns during her teaching experience. This added to her disillusionment with Christianity.

Ilavenil Meena Kandasamy is a writer and activist based in Tamil Nadu whose body of writing revolves around feminism and the anti-caste movements of the present day Indian milieu. Kandasamy has edited *The Dalit*, a bi-monthly English magazine sponsored by the Dalit Media Network. Kandasamy remains vocal about numerous contemporary political, social and economic issues relating to caste and women's rights in many ways. Through social media, she has managed to circulate her views in the public realm.She has been a columnist for platforms like *Outlook India*. Kandasamy has vehemently opposed academic language due to its provincialism and essentialist approach .She has advocated linguistic freedom through her poetry .Her poetry employs gynocritical view of the world. In the poem "One Eyed", she has highlighted the predicament of dalit women and the atrocities committed against them. Dhanam, a dalit woman was "torn in half"when she attempted to fetch a pot of water at the cost of her left eye

> ....the teacher sees a girl breaking the rule
> the doctor sees a medical emergency
> the school sees a potentialembarrassment
> the press sees a headline and a photofeature

dhanam sees a world torn in half
her left eye, lid open but light slapped away,
the price for a taste of that touchable water. (Priya, 293)

Kandasamy has condemned stereotypical roles assigned on the basis of caste and gender heirarchies. She recognises herself as a dalit feminist. Her novels have re-imagined Hindu and Tamil myths with the use of anti-caste perspective. Her fearless opposition to hierarchical structure of Hindu society has often been met with hatred and threats, especially on social media. However, she remains undeterred. Both Bama and Meena Kandasamy are public intellectuals. They have surpassed the barriers of gender and caste in their criticism of the hypocrisy of religious institutions. They are performing the dual task of being both a professional and activist. They refuse to accept phallocentric language of their male counterparts. Their gynocentric language is both unabashed and celebratory.Both of these dalit feminist writers commemorate their intellectual ancestors.

Bama's *Sangati* deals with the physical and mental ramifications of caste system. The novel encompasses several generations of women. Autobiographical tone of the novel enables finer understanding of the authorial intention. The novel is a collection of anecdotes and memories that represents the life of Paraiyar women in Tamil Nadu. All dalit women are financially dependent in the novel. They cannot exercise any authority over their own earnings. Through the character of Marriamma, the heinousness of sexual assault borne dalit women on a daily basis is reported by the author. The inability to successfully repel advances from affluent men stems from perennial poverty. Whipping, lynching and canning by fathers, husbands and brothers is an everyday occurrence in the lives of these women. Trauma is omnipresent in all individual accounts. Bama's use of language is different from other Indian writers. She uses the vernacular to describe events. Sharing is vital to the existence of women in this novel. They communicate both anger and pain to fellow women. The language is rife with sexual connotations which makes the novel liberating. Bama Says in her book Sangati, we must be strong. We must show by our own resolute lives that we believe ardently in our independence. I told myself that we must never allow our minds to be worn out, damaged, and broken in the belief that this is our fate, just as we work hard so long as there is strength in our bodies, so too, we must strengthen our hearts and minds in order to survive (Bama 59).

Meena Kandasamy's feminist rendering of James Joyce's *A Portrait of a Writer as a Young Man* has been published as *When I Hit You: Or, A Portrait of the Writer as a Young Wife*. Kandasamy has narrated the dehumanisation of Dalit wives and their struggle to both retain and also invent their identity. Narrator's husband, an educated professional gradually dominates every facet of her life, including her relationships with other people. The novel depicts how domestic abuse leads to isolation .Kandasamy's echt storytelling introduces the readers to her narrator's strategies of survival. Stalling pregnancy, drafting letters to imaginary lovers and remembering past dalliances form her defence mechanism. His violent behaviour eventually compels her to "climb into the incredible sadness of silence", meeting her husband's chief demand. Her robs her of her autonomy. She is stripped of self-expression. The novel makes a bold statement. It reminds its readers of the power of written word and warns the proponents of misogyny.

Works Cited

Bair, Deirdre. "Simone De Beauvoir: Politics, Language, and Feminist Identity." *Yale French Studies*, no. 72, 1986, pp. 149–162. *JSTOR*

Bama, Sangati.translated from Tamil by Lakshmi Holmstrom, Oxford University Press, New Delhi, 2005.

Barry, P 2009, Beginning theory; An introduction to literary and cultural theory, Manchester University Press, Manchester. Beauvoir, Simone de, et al. *The Second Sex*. Vintage Books, 2011.

Beauvoir, Simone de, et al. *The Second Sex*. Vintage Books, 2011.

Butler, Judith. "Performative Acts and Gender Constitution: An Essay in Phenomenology and Feminist Theory." *Theatre Journal*, vol. 40, no. 4, 1988, pp. 519–531. *JSTOR*, www.jstor.org/stable/3207893.

Faustina, Bama. Karukku: Trans. Laxmi Holmstrom, Oxford University Press: New Delhi, 2012.

Kandasamy, Meena. *When I Hit You, or, a Portrait of the Writer as a Young Wife.* Atlantic Books, 2018.

Kennamer, J.D (1990). "Self-serving biases in perceiving the opinions of others: Implications for the spiral of silence". *Communication Research.* 17 (3): 393–404.

King, Margaret Leah. "The Social Role if Intellectuals: Antonio Gramsci and the Italian Renaissance." *Soundings: An Interdisciplinary Journal,* vol. 61, no. 1, 1978, pp. 23–46. *JSTOR,* www.jstor.org/stable/41178047.

Priya, C. (2016). Predicament of Dalits in the Select Poems of Meena Kandasamy.

IRAInternational Journal of Management & Social Sciences (ISSN 2455-2267), 4(1). doi:http://dx.doi.org/10.21013/jmss.v4.n1.p24

Rege, S (1994): 'Caste and Gender :The Violence Against Women in India' in P Jogdand (ed), Dalit Women, Gyan, New Delhi. -(1995): 'Hegemonic Appropriation of Sexuality: The Case of the Erotic Lavani ofMaharashtra', Contributiolns to Intdian Sociology, Vol 29, Nos I anti 2.

Sharmila Rege. "Dalit Women Talk Differently: A Critique of 'Difference' and Towards a Dalit Feminist Standpoint Position." *Economic and Political Weekly,* vol. 33, no. 44, 1998, pp. WS39–WS46. *JSTOR,* www.jstor.org/stable/4407323.

Shils, Edward. "The Culture of the Indian Intellectual." *The Sewanee Review,* vol. 67, no. 3, 1959, pp. 401–421. *JSTOR,* www.jstor.org/stable/27538827.

Small, Helen. *The Public Intellectual.* Blackwell, 2002.

Thapar, Romila. "To Question or Not To Question?: That Is the Question." *Social Scientist,* vol. 42, no. 11/12, 2014, pp. 3–16. *JSTOR,* www.jstor.org/stable/24372899.

Tharu, Susie. "The Impossible Subject: Caste and the Gendered Body." *Economic and Political Weekly,* vol. 31, no. 22, 1996, pp. 1311–1315. *JSTOR,* www.jstor.org/stable/4404206.

Part - IV

Revisiting Silent Self(s): Engagement with Theory and Genre

1

Echoes of Silence in Time and Being: An Exploration of the Self in Silently Lived Lives

— *Gagandeep Kaur Ahluwalia*

Introduction

There is a look every girl inherits from her mother. A slight widening of the eyes, an infinitesimal shake of the head, and a tiny point of the chin— *Be Silent!*— it screams, ironically in silence. Every child knows that look, it speaks volumes. It speaks of coming disasters, of something terrifying bubbling inside the mother, in her imagination, or her perceived reality, a reality she was born in, raised in, lives in; a reality unlikely to change with the shifts in research or revelations in media or with social media hashtag campaigns. She is a woman who has power in her life—she is a daughter, a sister, a mother, a wife, a friend, a careerwoman—but she is not a person, not to the people who see her, perhaps not even to herself. These are silences that impact all lives, of men and women alike, of binary and non binary folx, across the lines drawn by men on land and sea, across generations, across time. There is a quiet voice inside that speaks to us sometimes, telling us to stay quiet, to make ourselves as small as possible, hope that we are invisible, and pray, pray this moment of terror passes. There is a silent caveat to keeping the self safe, *thou shalt not utter, even to oneself, if only internally, that which may break through and shatter the fragile realities we have constructed and live in.* This is a rule learned by terrified children of fearful mothers, by wives of terrifying husbands, by mothers of headstrong sons, by sons of docile mothers who grow up to be men, evident and visible and animated.

This paper is neither a deep dive into the theory of what makes silence so powerful and terrible, nor what gives it a kryptonite like quality. This paper is not a straight line from theory to interpretation. This paper is a fragment of a map of the selves we carry in us, hoping to find locators of selves and possibilities, in fact, it is a possibility in hope and in deed. This paper is a crack in a vacuum sealed room through which sound may escape.

The Silenced Self

There is very real space where we learn to react to certain triggers and it starts in utero. The foetus absorbs the mother's anxieties, her warmth, her feelings of quiet joy, her silence, her terrors and also feelings she cannot name or feel herself. How does one begin to articulate the unimagined—yet very real, strongly felt "somethings" that threaten to freeze us in place and flatten ourselves against the nearest hard plane, so as to let it pass? Why do we keep coming back to mothers, and by extension women? Because women are the carriers of multiverses and all these universes are alive inside of us at any given moment in space and time. Because biologically, women conceive and give birth to the young ones. The infants who carry us forward into the future sustain the hope for survival of the species. The genetic code in all of us is a combination of codes inherited by our parents, and theirs is an inheritance of their parents, and so on. Along with this genetic code, a blueprint of who we are, if you will, other things are also inherited. Things that define how we feel, how we construct a sense of who we are around what we are given, things that create for us, and destroy for us. Allow me to elaborate on the link between internalised patterns of a multitude of possible selves and the self that we become. A panopticon was a prison designed by social theorist Jeremy Bentham in the 18th century. Panopticon etymologically is derived from the Greek word *Panoptes* which means "all seeing". Bentham proposed a singular tower with one guard in it, built in a way that the guard can see into the cells, watch the prison inmates, but the prisoners do not know they are being watched. But is knowing limited to seeing or hearing? Knowing relies on evidence that theory often discards— *feelings*. The prickly sensation at the back of your neck, the discomfort that makes you squirm, that feeling you cannot shake—being observed, watched makes your entire body wake up and scream. But Bentham's Panopticon brings to us Foucault's *Panopticism* which is a way for political power to insert itself inside our lives, for power to penetrate our bodies and pierce our skins and reside inside us so we continue to behave correctly. This *correctness* is in question here. We inherit the rules for correctness and docility in utero. We may be alive in a time that is different from when those rules came into being, but we stick to them anyway because we don't seem to know any better. Even if one assumes, we know a different truth, that we are attempting to speak it, our bodies begin to feel incorrect when we deny the loud internal voices of our others screaming at us to follow, be correct again, be docile, be silent. That guard in the tower we cannot see is a constant trigger for our bodies to remain vigilant, to remain alive to the possibility of punishment if we so much as put a shadow of a toe across the line. That internalised guard is asking us, silently, to mind ourselves, our bodies, our feelings, our very existence so as to not be a source of discomfiture to the "Other". It goes on in silence for so long, we no longer know where we begin and the Other ends. We cyclically continue to other our selves, we continue to raise our babies to be others, to themselves and to external others. We no longer can trace that singular thread that tells us the story of our self, without being knotted with other threads that often distract us and lead us down pathways to alternate universes that exist as we exist, we inhabit them all at once, weaving in and out of possible lives and possible people that we are and are not. Who hears these many voices, silently waiting for their turn, these people rendered mute by the silence of the "Other"? Certainly, not us.

Our souls are marked by the invisible prison we carry around with us. A prison where authenticity is in question. Foucault would say, "the soul is the prison of the body." There are multiple subjectivities that are actively engaged inside a person at any given time. These different subjective positions are not only culturally contextualised, but are also dictated by the social position occupied by a person's body(male or female), that body's position in the family hierarchy (Son vs Son-in-law, Daughter vs Daughter-in-law etc.), and that family's position in the class and caste system of social organisation. These are further complicated by the lived-in geographical location of the person. There is a history of postulating a theory of the psyche keeping at the centre of it, the White European Imperial Man, effectively invisibilising the subaltern (any *other* man), and completely decimating the subaltern of the subaltern (the other of the othered man, the woman). The factual truth is that as a woman born in an erstwhile colony of the White European Imperial Man, I carry a history in my blood. Blood which runs in my veins, is borrowed from my mother in her womb, who borrowed hers from her mother, who borrowed blood from hers and it goes back like that for generations that I cannot even trace. This blood carries my history, it carries an identity, it carries in it the impossible, irradiated truth—I exist in noughts, *not* white, *not* man, *not enough.* In asking for a truth, we often misguidedly rely on what is seen, and knowledge of the thing-as-it-is is relegated to a footnote of a thesis that emphasises the realness of that which can be seen. Before one can embark on the search for a truth, one must be made aware of one's own simulated existence—that which is created by assuming that the difference in the locatedness of a theory, a concept, a philosophy, or a person does not alter the truth. That it does not indeed put a magical spell on it and make it appear as something else, that the imaginary does not suddenly become too real, and that real then embarks on a mission of finding *the* truth, which is ultimately false but appears real. Thus is born the mystified past, a past that is methodically explored and investigated, corroborated and researched, and a 'truth' is discovered. But who's truth is this? Who's search for truth or meaning in this? And who is answering these silent pleas for meaning, for a tether, for a root, for a *voice?* Having a voice does not come with the condition of being heard. Being heard does not come with the guarantee of meaning being made. Having a body does not automatically create a person—in our minds or an other's.

The story of the woman is a complex concoction of history, development, profound change and contradictions. One often wonders how modernity has affected the experience of being for anyone who identifies as female. In 1750s England, the word for a woman who was intellectual, and wished for, or thought of things other than the home and hearth was "bluestocking" which was used only in a derogatory way. A woman who dared to stake claim on her husband's property after he died and started a literary society for women in an era where traditionally women were prevented from gaining education was a bluestocking, and other women were encouraged by their men to not engage with these women. The British East India Company got here in early 17th century, company rule started in the mid-18th century and a full century later, British Raj of the Crown was established circa 1858, the year the first Government of India Act was passed. It begs one to question how much the British brought over in terms of culture and tradition onto the land that they had freshly colonised in order to bring culture to the native. Indian women exist in paradoxes: men worship goddesses, but rape women, beat their wives, kill their infant daughters. Looking at it historically, this paradoxical existence's foundation can be found in the Aryan history. Determined to keep themselves separate from the indigenous tribes of India, the Aryans put together a system which became the ground work for the caste system that still prevails in our country. The account of women's status in the *Rig Veda,* as left by the Aryans is not so depreciated. Over the next two thousand years, girls were married off at a very young age, were barred from religious rituals, widows weren't permitted to remarry. It got to a point where an autonomous life for a woman was a distant dream. The theory here is that, as we progressed from a tribal, nomadic society to a sedentary one; the roles of women changed which affected their position in society. Manu writes that a woman is as foul as a falsehood. His codified laws first and foremost set down the rules of caste in India, to keep the 'outsiders' in their places. Consequently, there are strict rules about who may marry whom; for these rules to be effective women had to be controlled thereby causing massive deterioration of their place in society. The question then here is how do we strike a balance between our culture that is five thousand years old, and our seventy two year old nation; between tradition and modernity, between all those binaries that seem to dictate an existence so unique, so Indian? To think about women and their relationship with their own bodies, their existence as non-primary beings in their lives and in the world, their ways to navigate the world of man, is a cultural undertaking that involves sociocultural and anthropological elements to be weaved in the psychoanalytic discourse of femaleness of being.

Femaleness in Being

"It's a man's world", goes the song. Even though James Brown follows it up with "But it would be nothing without a woman or a girl", he is using the woman as an ornamental piece, something that completes the picture, but is not necessary to the man in this picture. That is also the problem with theorising womanhood, or female personhood in this world. How is femininity constructed by men, and how it is constructed by female persons and their lived experiences don't fully fit into structured or unstructured research. Precisely because it is a man's world. A woman's world is structurally different, it consists of fears—of public spaces, of female bodies being attacked, of having a voice and opinion that if in contrast with a man, invites threats of violence. A woman's world is consistently anxious. Her expression of feelings is "that time of the month", or period anxiety — getting it on time, not getting it on time, a stain in a public space, the opinions of others all these are constantly thrown as measurers of her worth. The Indian woman exists in a perpetual Have/Hold discursive binary: a virgin and a whore, a wife and a mistress (Wendy Hollway). There is no part of our lives as women, where we are not performing. Our girlhoods, young adulthoods, and later years are all spent performing an idea of being, an idea of the other and we raise our daughters to be performers too. The correctness of femaleness is in this performance. The correctness of woman is in this performance of femininity. Any woman who uses this performance to carve out an identity, a self that does not fit into the preapproved pattern is then deemed incorrect. Kakar writes about how a woman maintains power over the family and household if she bears a son, a woman with daughters on the other hand is reduced in power and value. Femaleness is less, even to the woman. It is a 'fate' one must learn to make the best of. Yet, culturally, a woman's vagina is the place where izzat of the *khandan* of men resides. Her body is a battleground for piousness, for purity, for claim to power, and for social position, and for power. But her voice, her voice is an inconvenience. A voice is used to express contentment, and also discontent. So is her silence. If she uses her voice to ask for what she needs, deserves, wants—she is too much. If she uses her voice to report her hurt, her sadness, her disappointments—she is too much. If she uses her voice to speak for herself—she is too much. Her needs, her desires are an inconvenience. She must not be heard, and should be seen only when relevant. If she stays silent—why did she not say anything: No one asked her to suffer in silence. If she uses her silence to convey her feelings—she is barbaric, making the other suffer like that. Silence is uncomfortable. Human beings are all about making discomfort go away. Today, when we have female CEOs, astronauts, professors, bankers and what not—these are still women raised in a gendered position, with roles, duties, shoulds and should nots built in, with performativity plugged into the very subatomic particles of personhood. External reality has to be acquired by all individuals. Three processes happen that are effective in silencing the female psyche: (1) The child becomes a perfectly rational adult child, (2) it becomes the absent centre of a world of other people, and (3) the child is seen only as others relate to it. There is an absence of a true self that tethers us to ourselves, an absence of a skin that contains all our multiverses from exploding out of us, an absence of language with which gaps in the experience of the self can be interpreted and understood.

To conclude, I offer more of my words, and some parts of me, uttered and written in silence by me, in verse.

Throbbing, there.
Scratching at my throat to get out
Not a scream
But a lifetime of cuts
Itchy scabs and welts on my soul
Rubbing soft flesh
Against sandpaper people
Trying to rid myself of
Generations of itches
Running through my veins
Under my skin,
Inside it, clawing to get out
Between bone and muscle
Are stories scratched
On bodies of women who
Gave birth to me
My skin is full
There is no space for
My stories, my sex,
My self - your touch,
To carve a new wound

To nurse it and dress it
To find a new itch and
Scratch it, bleed it
I'm still walking through
A prickly forest
Of my mother's and her mother's and her mother's feelings
I duck, I slither, I wobble
I fall
The pricking doesn't stop
My skin is dotted with
Perfect wounds,
A wall full of accolades
Of sons birthed and grown,
Aesthetically appealing
Making me grotesquely
Beautiful
my legacy is of
Perfect wounds never healing
Feminine voices never screaming
Rough possessive hands
Never touching
Always touching
Binding, Penetrating,
Controlling.
Give me up to breathe
Air that drowns my lungs
In hot tar and sulphur
Until I petrify
New stories I make
Bake inside the demon sludge
I am made of.

It burns you.
Me, I am perfect,
Don't you know?

Works Cited

Baudrillard, Jean. "Simulacra And Simulations". *Jean Baudrillard, Selected Writings*, 1988, Accessed 18 Oct 2019.

Brox, Jane. "The Silence Of Women". *Longreads*, 2019, https://longreads.com/2019/01/15/the-silence-of-women/.

Das, Veena, and Stanley Cavell. *Life And Words*. Univ. Of California Press, 2008.

Foucault, Michel. *Discipline And Punish*. Vintage Books, 1977.

Greenfield, Rebecca, and Janet Paskin. "The True Cost Of Women's Silence". *Bloomberg.Com*, 2018, https://www.bloomberg.com/news/articles/2018-09-27/the-true-cost-of-unreported-sexual-harassment.

Gyllenhaal, Kathleen M. "In Utero". *In Utero*, 2016, https://www.inuterofilm.com/. Accessed 17 Oct 2019.

Kakar, Sudhir. *Culture And Psyche*. Oxford University Press, 2009.

Kakar, Sudhir, and Katharina Kakar. *The Indians*. Penguin, Viking, 2007.

Quintana, Suzanna. "The Cultural Silencing Of Women". *Medium*, 2018, https://medium.com/publishous/the-cultural-silencing-of-women-94f27fbb7ef1.

Solnit, Rebecca. "Silence And Powerlessness Go Hand In Hand – Women'S Voices Must Be Heard | Rebecca Solnit". *The Guardian*, 2017, https://www.theguardian.com/commentisfree/2017/mar/08/silence-powerlessness-womens-voices-rebecca-solnit.

Spivak, Gayatri Chakravorty. "Can The Subaltern Speak". *Marxism And The Interpretation Of Culture*, Cary Nelson and Larry Grossberg, 1988, Accessed 18 Oct 2019.

Spivak, Gayatri Chakravorty. "Psychoanalysis In The Left Field And Fieldworking". *Speculations After Freud*, Sonu Shamdasani and Michael Munchow, Routledge, 2002, Accessed 18 Oct 2019.

Thapar, Romila. *A History Of India*. Penguin Books, 1992.

2

Autobiography as Resistance: Marjane Satrapi

— Nilanjana Ray

Gillian Whitlock terms autobiography as a "soft weapon" and how it has the power to "personalize and humanize categories of people whose experiences are frequently unseen and unheard." In making her observation, she was referring to the mode of autobiography acting as a potent way of self-expression for displaced and marginalized communities from conflict-ridden places like Iraq, Baghdad, Iran etc and how such narratives are produced specifically for "mass market readerships in the West". She elaborates on her use of the term "soft weapon":

> It is a "soft" weapon because it is easily co-opted into propaganda. In modern democratic societies propaganda is frequently not the violent and coercive imposition of ideas but a careful manipulation of opinion and emotion in the public sphere and a management of information in the engineering of consent. Life narrative can be complicit in these processes.

Life narratives written by women seek to erase and re-interpret the identity ascribed to them. When it comes to re-imagining trauma in women's life writing, the graphic novel has emerged as a powerful mode of narration and autobiography in terms of redefining the "self". In conditions of modernity, the idea and sense of the "self" are increasingly precarious. Trauma hits at the essence of a person's being and causes her/him to revaluate the terms of self-identity. The form of the autobiography becomes a way of reviving the past and performs the function of wish-fulfilment. In the backdrop of this observation, this paper aims to discuss and analyse Marjane Satrapi's graphic novels *Persepolis* and *Embroideries* as feminist modes of self-expression that defy silence and censorship.

For Satrapi, her series of autobiographical graphic novels is a way of depicting her childhood, negotiating her privileged class position and revisiting her life before she became an Iranian expat during the Islamic Revolution in 1979 and finally a resident of France. Her mode of storytelling involves using recurrent symbols and motifs expressed in a simple black and white panelling. Each of her novels deal with a specific aspect of her life and while *Persepolis* is about the onset of the Islamic Revolution and her escape from the country and eventual return, only to leave again, *Embroideries* offers a glimpse into the private lives of Iranian women, centred around Marjane's grandmother, mother and their friends. The genre of war comics journalism involves writers like Joe Sacco and Guy Delisle who provide objective details on conflict between the state and its people, but people like Satrapi depict a personal and insider's view of what it's like to be a refugee, of leaving behind a life that seems to have been an illusion. Interestingly enough, Satrapi's novels lie at the intersection of trauma and autobiography represented through a child's perspective. As an Iranian immigrant living in France, these texts are a "memory object" that retrace her roots to an Iran that was her safe haven and made her who she is.

Picturing Time in Panels

The medium of the graphic novel attains documentary value because of its manipulation of frames called "gutters" that allows for a simultaneous fluid and static narration, thereby allowing space for feminist modes of subjective aesthetic reproduction. In *Persepolis* Satrapi depicts herself in the novel as a young girl and coupled with the minimalist style, successfully erases the boundaries between an "Other" Iranian girl and the reader.

Persepolis opens with the chapter titled "The Veil" and there's a feeling of actually peering into Marjane's life from under a veil. The first two panels of the first chapter establish her individuality amidst the row of similar looking veiled girls, and immediately one has to take this figure as the commanding voice. The straightforward, systematic progress of the novel depicted in continuous rectangular panels with similarly shaped speech boxes is in stark contrast to the tumultuous life that the author, and the main protagonist of the novel, Marji, has. Unlike *The Diary of Anne Frank*, which was meant to be a private document, and bears very little contact of the protagonist with the outside world, *Persepolis* depicts the life of an Iranian girl who was among those lucky few to have escaped the troubled homeland. The change from a liberal Iranian society to one controlled by a regressive dictum is expressed using a montage-like sequence of images that depict the lives of the narrator and the people around her. The defiant spirit that runs throughout the novel is a statement against the portrayal of post 1979 Iranians as submissive citizens meekly accepting the terms of survival as dictated by a fundamentalist government. Satrapi goes against the dominant non-fiction narrative styles of violent rhetoric and political blame games. Instead, she depicts how any country can become Iran, how many Marjis can't afford to escape. Her criticism of the State is strictly through the young Marji, which gives it a subtle tone. The alarming situation of the Revolution is defused by the young Satrapi with her innocent remarks like, "The Revolution is like a bicycle. When the wheels don't turn, it falls." (10).

Until the moment Marji leaves, the speech bubbles between she and her parents become lesser. Her grandmother is brought in, who stays with them, completes the family picture and weaves the three generations together for that final night before Marji leaves. At the airport, her father imparts a final advice: "You've got to go now. Don't forget who you are and where you come from." (152). It echoes the sentiment of every immigrant, looking for steady ground in unknown lands. This is a reminder of their past, the history, and the memories which has no existence to the outer world. Their identities are determined by their nationality, their religion and their overall status of being an "outsider". Much of the literature and information on historical events like the World Wars, Holocaust, and the Armenian Genocide are in the form of statistics, documents, pity evoking photographs, documentaries, books written from these sources and other such mainstream forms of archiving and documentation. Sometimes it just remains a box of unopened files and papers. *Persepolis* differs by offering a 10 year old girl's perspective of what she had seen, heard and now remembers, in an entirely different format and a genre of its own. She not only contributes to a global repository of visual archives on events that changed geopolitics forever, but also re-lives her experiences in a world which hasn't really changed much.

Trauma of war and victimhood has found unique modes of self-expression, the graphic novel being one of the most popular ones in the last thirty years, beginning with the path-breaking *Maus* by Art Spiegelman. With the publication *Maus*, the notion of graphic novels being exclusively a young male's domain changed. The minimalist black and white style used by Satrapi in all her novels normalizes trauma and implies that the "historically traumatic doesn't have to be visually traumatic" (Chute, 135). The fragmented nature of storytelling involved in comics and graphic novels bear testimony to the pattern of remembering traumatic memories.

Unlike *Persepolis*, *Embroideries* has a lack of strict panel details or even speech bubbles. Such a counter approach to traditional formats of graphic novels makes this a revolutionary text not bound by strictures of the methods of storytelling. The content of this novel – erotic lives of Iranian women under the shackles of patriarchy and fundamentalism that foment a culture of controlling women's bodies and lives- fits in perfectly with the underground subculture from which the genre of comics and later on graphic novels emerged from, and goes well with the hidden and rebellious private lives of many Iranian women like the ones talked about in this novel. The absence of panel details opens up the text to the possibility of juxtaposing the past and present, leading to a rupture in the way time is constricted in the space of a few panels and in between them, i.e., in the "gutters". There is a flow of conversation and unrestricted access to private lives of women and this creates a space of relief and freedom for these women, each of who have suffered some degree of oppression including forced marriages, marital rape and even surgeries to remain youthful mistresses. Porosity of these boundaries makes this novel a memoir with its voices rooted in a multitude, a collective. The child's perspective here gets validated by the other adult women present in the scene and creates a therapeutic safe space for emotional release.

Samovar, Cigarettes and Sex

Unlike the darker images of Phoebe Gloeckner in her works like *The Diary of a Teenage Girl* that have a consistent backdrop of coming to terms with trauma, *Embroideries* talks about sexuality in an intimate and friendly space consisting of women of different ages, sharing their own set of experiences in a very light hearted manner. After the Islamic Revolution of 1979, new fundamentalist rules about public morality and choices were enforced and deviants were flogged along with jail time. In the backdrop of such a repressive and anti-feminist socio-political space, the women need a safe haven to discuss their lives. Satrapi sets the stage for these women by painting the scene with the piping hot fumes from the samovar and the opium of her grandmother, both necessary for engaging in enlightening conversation. While Marjane's grandmother was married thrice, one of her friends indulged in trickery to avoid being detected of having a past sexual relationship. When the women share their stories and discuss about other women and their ordeals, one gets a sense of the prevailing double standards of morality and how they are enforced as a means to only control and manipulate women's bodies. The stories and anecdotes are shared by all the women present there including a young Marjane, and this presence of at least three different generations of women with their tales speaks of a circular nature of history and time, a breakdown in the walls of objectified history controlled only by a select group of people. As with *Persepolis*, Satrapi depicts herself in the novel as a young girl and coupled with the minimalist style, successfully erases the boundaries between an "other" Iranian girl and a reader, thereby removing class and ethnic specificities and driving home the normal about Iranian upbringing, a kind of counter-approach to the images and stereotypes propagated by American media about Iranian women and the country in general. While explicit discussions take place among the women, one can't help but notice the striking absence of any explicit imagery, except in one page where a cheating husband is shown engaging sexually with Marjane's grandmother's friend, but there's no nudity involved. This makes her novels different from Phoebe Gloeckner and Aline Kominsky-Crumb who deal with sexual violence and trauma in their works, with explicit depiction that attest to the sense of shock that characterised the actual events. Instead of fulfilling a very mainstream cultural expectation of displaying an objectified male phallus in *Embroideries*, the author chooses to only suggest it. The feminist aspect of this novel lies in how much the narrative discloses meaning without being explicit and the control it exerts on how bodies are viewed in the public discourse.

Embroidering Selves and Stories

The title of the novel is derived from a surgery that women all over the world undergo to avoid being detected of their loss of virginity. The colloquial term for that surgery being used as the title of the novel shows how Satrapi has brought out the intensely private and even profane to the public domain and redefined how it is viewed. This is her way of etching the history of her women, their lives and untold stories.

An embroidery as a piece of heirloom acts as material memory. It bears testimony to craftsmanship and makes it an artefact bearing the history of lived experiences. The woven thread and other intricate details sets apart different kinds of embroideries and are often handed down as part of a tradition. In light of this role played by a piece of embroidery, Satrapi's novel puts together myriad hues of these women's lives and presents readers with an object of memory that attests to its intention of effacing and redefining the connotations of sexuality.

In this process of stitching stories of all those women, Satrapi ascribes new identities where there were none. Her art of resistance lies in forging new identities and representing her past to a global audience that largely misunderstands her roots, her people.

Post-Revolution and Now

Jasmin Darznik, Iranian-American poet and novelist of two New York Times bestsellers, has observed that this profusion of Iranian narratives in the form of memoirs available in mass markets has sparked debates in America regarding who has the right to represent what exactly happened in the run up to the coup, the Islamic Revolution and the Iran-Iraq War. She observes that in the race for the right to represent, a crucial aspect of these memoirs is being overlooked- the Iranian woman's control over how she is represented and in what capacity. The strain of "Never forget" that runs through all of Satrapi's novels speaks volumes about the act of resistance and rebellion that informs such autobiographical life-writing. The mode of the graphic novel with its intensely personal form that consists of hand-drawn caricatures and text offers a more intimate encounter with the author who is actually in the process of drawing multiple fragmented selves.

New Modes of Writing Resistance

As a movement of resistance and defiance, the mode of autobiography does well to express marginalized identities. The form of the graphic novel, with its roots in cave paintings and tapestries, has a rich and evolving legacy that attests to the developing forms of feminist modes of production. Even though this format of the novel is widely seen as a mass market and capitalist product meant for a class specific readership that can afford to buy graphic novels, this postmodern form of the book with its combination of images and text has scope in influencing emergent readership about the various modes of self-expression that arise out of spaces of conflict. Such alternative modes of writing history are important to enrich literary historiography and provide a space of dissent and debate. This genre revels in its complexity to depict multiple complex themes wrapped in its ambiguity. Such an ambiguity opens the genre of autobiography in graphic novels to depict multiple fragmented selves and exert control. The making of the "life space" that has been pursued with the aid of memory is an energetic procedure during which the past is broken down, interpreted, re-evaluated, and reconstructed as a personal truth which is as firm and conclusive for the narrating "I" as existence itself. Memory is thus a major question for autobiography. Memory is the construction material for the author/narrator. Even if their research extends to documents, photographs and testimonies from others, everything will be filtered through the prism of the memory of the writing "I". This is not to say that a new personality –or a new person– has been created via the process of autobiography. It is more to say that the narrator/author has by the completion of an autobiography created a methodology –a theory– about interpreting (and through interpretation, understanding) their life. Putting oneself into an autobiographical narration is by default an attempt to carve a personal history. During this process, the author has to reinvent not only their own persona, but everybody else's too (parents, children, friends, enemies) and install them into history– which demands that they reinvent history as well. In the graphic medium the author creates the historical and visual context in a complex language, which can exploit oral and visual memories, is a product of research and remembering. The interaction between image, word and text creates a meta fictional narrative that fuses the personal with the political and creates a new aesthetic of resistance and protest.

Works Cited

Chute, Hillary L. *Disaster Drawn: Visual Witness, Comics, and Documentary Form*. The Belknap Press of Harvard UP, 2016.

--, --. *Graphic Women: Life Narrative and Contemporary Comics*. Columbia UP, 2010.

Darznik, Jasmin. "The Perils and Seductions of Home: Return Narratives of the Iranian Diaspora." *MELUS*, vol. 33, no. 2, 2008, pp. 55–71. *JSTOR*, www.jstor.org/stable/20343466.

Karim, Persis M., and Nasrin Rahimieh. "Introduction: Writing Iranian Americans into the American Literature Canon." *MELUS*, vol. 33, no. 2, 2008, pp. 7–16. *JSTOR*, www.jstor.org/stable/20343463.

Kirshenblatt-Gimblett, Barbara. "Objects of Memory: Material Culture as Life Review." *Folk Groups and Folklore Genres: A Reader*, edited by Elliott Oring, Utah State University Press, 1989.

Knowles, Sam. "The Postcolonial Graphic Novel and Trauma: From Maus to Malta". *Postcolonial Traumas: Memory, Narrative and Resistance*, edited by Abigail Ward, Palgrave Macmillan, 2015.

Satrapi, Marjane. *Persepolis*. Vintage, 2008.

Satrapi, Marjane. *Embroideries*. Jonathan Cape, 2008.

Whitlock, Gillian. "Word made flesh". *Soft Weapons Autobiography*. The University of Chicago Press, 2007.

3

Articulating Silence: A Postmodern Appropriation

— ***Ruchi Nagpal***

"McLuhan heralds the end of print; the Gutenberg galaxy burns itself out. Electric technology can dispense with words, and language can be shunted on the way to universal consciousness... At a certain limit of contemporary vision, language moves towards silence. Criticism must learn this to acknowledge this metaphor."
— **Ihab Hassan,** Metaphors of Silence (1)

Silence has often been endowed as the repository of great power which can transcend discourses if manifested in a radically revolutionized manner. Silence has a unique place in literature as philosophers, thinkers and writers since time immemorial have tried to problematize and redefine the concept of silence which in its most basic form would mean an abstinence from communication. At times a moment of complete stillness or a deliberate attempt to cease all communication qualifies as silence. But literature has always tried to probe deeper and the attempts have been made to articulate the repressed, the silenced thereby unleashing a plethora of discourses, voices and ideas which change the course of the day. The idea of silence has forever been there but every age has tried to play around it and redefine it through the politics of the times and epoch that constitutes it. The concern of the current paper is to look at the postmodern appropriation of the idea of silence which not only gets reiterated and redefined but it rather challenges the idea of 'voicing out the silence' and makes a case for a silence which is manifested through sublime and which not only transgresses the sphere of silence but also transcends the notion of articulation.

The idea often accentuated with silence is one of breaking the shackles and giving voice. The discourse of articulation has been popularized vis-à-vis silence which contests for coming to the fore and articulating the long silenced voices thereby giving them recognition and power. Corollary a nexus has been developed between the idea of power and the idea of articulation which stands in juxtaposition with silence. Contrary to this the concern of the current paper is to enunciate a discourse which resides in silence and transcends the domain through silence and not through articulation or voice per se.

Sublime thus becomes that category through which one could deliberate upon the idea of silence which becomes more convoluted and more powerful in its rendition. The concept of sublime is a long standing concept in literature which has been deliberated upon by thinkers since the time of Dionysius as some records show that the most ancient script on sublime which is "On The Sublime" is probably not the work of Cassius Longinus, a third century rhetorician but rather this text was composed by Dionysius of Halicarnassus. In this work Longinus examines man's ability through feeling and words, to reach beyond the realm of the human condition into greater mystery. The crux of the text however or the idea behind sublime which Longinus tries to define and explore tells us that by nature, sublime is "produced by greatness of soul, imitation, or imagery," cannot be contained in words, and Longinus often refers to its heights as reached by journey, or flight: "For, as if instinctively, our soul is uplifted by the true sublime; it takes a proud flight, and is filled with joy and vaunting, as though it had itself produced what it has heard." Originated or first discussed by Longinus, this idea was further developed by the likes of Edmund

Burke, Fredrick Schiller, Immanuel Kant and Jean Francois Lyotard. Longinus' idea however was completely different from what we understand it today. According to Longinus, sublime was a quality that could occur in any type of discourse, whether poetry or prose. He defined the effect of the sublime to be such which transports the reader, a passage that exercises irresistible domination over him and "shatters the subject like a bolt of lightning". For Longinus therefore, sublime resided in the capabilities of the speaker or the writer. The idea has been greatly modified since his time and Edmund Burk in his highly influential *Philosophical Inquiry into the Origin of our Ideas of the Sublime and Beautiful* published in 1757, attributes the eminence of sublime to the source which are "in any sort terrible" and his idea of sublime which differs from that of Longinus paves a path for the latter rendering of the concept by Kant in the Romantic and Lyotard in the postmodern age. Burke in defining sublime connects it to the concept of vastness in terms dimension or quantity. And his examples thus include vast architectural structures, Milton's description of Satan in *Paradise Lost* and natural phenomenon. The sublime passion, he says may be produced by "the noise of vast characters, raging storms, thunder or artillery," all of which evoke "a great and awful sensation in the mind". This idea of "great and awful sensation" vis-à-vis sublime finds prominence in the 18th century Romantic Movement where it reaches its height through the work of Immanuel Kant who in his *Critique of Judgment* discusses the idea in great detail along the same lines.

However it is the postmodern appropriation of the idea of sublime which connects it to the idea of silence and makes a case for something which becomes powerful in remaining silent more forcefully than ever. Jean Francois Lyotard one the "most notorious of the postmodern thinkers" in the words of Simon Tormey develops the idea of postmodernism and the art thereof. In his theorizations upon postmodernism, Lyotard makes a case for sublime by stating that postmodern art is manifested through sublime rather than through words and artifacts. And in taking the discourse of sublime and silence further, Lyotard gives an idea of postmodernism which defies straitjacketing and transcends all the definitional parameters. In defining the postmodern discourse and art, Lyotard writes:

> The postmodern would be that which, in the modern, puts forward the unpresentable in presentation itself; that which denies itself the solace of good forms, the consensus of a taste which would make it possible to share collectively the nostalgia for the unattainable; that which searches for new presentations, not in order to enjoy them but in order to impart a stronger sense of the unpresentable. (Lyotard, 81)

Lyotard makes a case for sublime wherein the cognitive apparatus which defines beauty as a synthesis of the faculty of perception and faculty of presentation defines sublime as something that the cognitive apparatus perceives but fails to represent and this failure becomes the most explicit feature of sublime. Rendering the postmodern art in the domain of sublime Lyotard enunciates a discourse which foregrounds silence in its most magnificent form. Mind perceives but fails to represent and upshot is both pleasure and pain which Lyotard defines as the ultimate experience of sublime. Failure of the cognitive apparatus to represent what it could perceive transcends the borderline of articulation and leaves the art in a domain where its most exclusive feature becomes its silence and it communicates through silence by taking recourse in sublime.

Lyotard goes back to Immanuel Kant and his *Critique of Judgment* wherein Kant defines Sublime as this peculiar amalgamation of fear and pleasure which in its entirety escapes representation. "The sublime feeling is therefore a kind of rapid alternation between the fear of the overwhelming and the peculiar pleasure of seeing that overwhelming overwhelmed." Sublime is contained in a very subjective experience determined by a certain relationship between power of reason and the power of imagination. Kantian definition or enunciation of aesthetics happens primarily through the idea of unavailability and therefore Malevich's art work becomes a prime example which concocts the idea of silence with sublime to render a powerful and challenging work of art. Kazimir Malevich was a Russian Avant-Garde artist and art theorist who made Suprematist Composition: White on White in 1918 which was abstract oil on canvas painting:

> Part of a series of white on white works begun by Malevich in 1916, the work depicts a white square, portrayed off centre and at an angle on a ground which is also a white square of a slightly warmer tone. The work measures 79.5 by 79.5 centimetres (31.3 in × 31.3 in). Malevich dispenses with most of the characteristics of representational art, with no sense of colour, depth, or volume, leaving a simple monochrome geometrical shape, not precisely symmetrical, with imprecisely defined boundaries. Although the artwork is stripped of most detail, brush strokes are evident in this painting and the artist tried to make it look as if the tilted square is coming out of the canvas. Malevich intended the painting to evoke a feeling of floating, with the colour white symbolizing infinity, and the slight tilt of the square suggests movement. (Wikipedia, white on white) Various ideas and theories related to this work of art suggest that the painter wished to articulate something immense, "a feeling of floating" and yet the literal understanding of the work would make a case for the fact that the artist has stripped the art work to nothing. Invoking a strong feeling through nothing which has latent ideas embedded in it is what calls for the aesthetic of sublime. In Kant's view, the experience of the sublime manifests on the one "its pre-eminence over nature," even when confronted by the "immeasurability" of nature's magnitude and the "irresistibility" of its might.

The Lyotardian idea of silence and sublime could not be confused with 'lack' because he attributes really productive and powerful potential to sublime and doesn't seem to say that it's a sweet nothing thereby furthering the postmodern ambiguity. In the words of Simon Tormey:

> The 'reality' in which Lyotard was interested was not an absence or 'lack' which could be constructed through gap between the language and the world it seeks to 'represent'. Rather, he was interested in exploring the space between the perceptions of something and its symbolization, the implication being that there were things we could perceive but not articulate: sensations, experiences and feelings that could not be reduced to words, but which might, in contrast express themselves in art. Language, he wanted to say, is not all that there is; and all there is could not be rendered in language. In *Discourse, Figures*, he argues that the world is constructed 'in language'; but- contra Derrida and others- in some sense the world resists reduction to language. (Tormey, 154)

This very idea which takes the Lyotardian discourse beyond linguistic and paralinguistic elements into the domain of sublime wherein meaning happens beyond language is what connects it to the notion of silence per se which becomes radical in transcending the linguistic domain that claims symbolization through this semiotic medium. It foregrounds the Lyotardian idea that "perception cannot be reduced to language or symbolization and thus only accessible in an extra linguistic fashion" (Tormey, 153).

Lyotard not only develops the aesthetics of postmodern sublime vis-à-vis postmodern literature and theory but he also politicizes the very idea of postmodern by passing it over in the domain of silence which when amalgamated with sublime becomes one of the most radical characteristic of the postmodern art. Lyotard in his essay "Answering the Question: What is Postmodernism", writes, "The work of Proust and that of Joyce both allude to something which does not allow itself to be made present. Allusion, to which Paolo Fabbri recently called by attention, is perhaps a form of expression indispensible to the works which belong to an aesthetic of the sublime" (Lyotard, 80).

It is this fore grounding of the idea of silence with sublime which makes postmodern radical as well as indefinable. The revolt becomes all the more powerful and assertive when the silence becomes pregnant with sublime, which in its enunciation and experience unleashes the most radical and subversive of the discourse. An example could be given, though highly philosophical and theoretical it makes an attempt to familiarize the readers with the concept of sublime in more practical terms. Visiting a sea shore at night and experiencing the waves coming and going would put the individual in an ambiguous position where the idea of fear would overpower the individual since the sea and waves have the power to erase the existence of the individual from the face of the earth in a second without leaving behind any trace whatsoever and at the same time the grandeur of nature gives the individual a pleasurable feeling wherein he tries to comprehend the vastness and grandness of the sea itself. In that very moment when the individual experiences both pleasure and pain is both terrified and joyous is when he encounters the feeling of sublime in the most silent manner possible. Nature articulates its power and grandeur through silence which leads to the ultimate feeling of sublime. In the words of Fredrick Schiller, "It is a combination of woefulness, which expresses itself in its highest degree as a shudder, and of joyfulness, which can rise up to enrapture, and, although it is not properly pleasure, is yet widely preferred to every pleasure by fine souls" (Schiller, 5).

And thus the most powerful rendition of the concept is available in Lyotard's *Differend* wherein he explains that the differend is a state in which something cannot be put into phrases, something is essentially silent and yet this 'something' is felt as a call to invent new phrases by means of which it can be expressed and yet it the expression lacks total comprehensibility. The postmodern appropriation of the concept of silence thus becomes an endless play of comprehension through linguistic as well as paralinguistic mediums which thwart the category altogether by becoming more powerful with sublime and rendering the idea of meaning in the linguistic sense asunder thereby opening new horizons for the very idea of silence.

Works Cited

Fitz, Earl E. "A Discourse of Silence: The Postmodernism of Clarice Lispector." Contemporary Literature, vol. 28, no. 4, 1987, pp. 420- 436, JSTOR, www.jstor.org/stable/1208309.

Hutcheon, Linda. Poetics of Postmodernism: History, Theory, Fiction. Taylor and Francis e-Library, 2014, pp. 23.

Kant, Immanuel. Critique of Judgment. Translated by Werner S. Pluher, Hackett Publishing Company, 1790, pp. 227.

Lyotard, Jean Francois. "Answering the Question: What is Postmodernism?" The Postmodern Condition: A Report on Knowledge, translated by Geoff Bennigton et al., Theory and History of Literature, vol.10, Manchester UP, 1984, pp. 71-82.

Lyotard, Jean Francois. "The Sublime and the Avant- Garde". *The Bloomsbury Anthology of Aesthetics,* 1948.

Lyotard, Jean Francois. *The Differend: Phrases in Dispute.* University of Minnesota Press, 1988.

Longinus on the Sublime, translated by W. Rhys Roberts (London: Cambridge University Press, 1899).

Schiller, Fredrick. "On the Sublime". Schiller institute.https://schillerinstitute.com/

Simons, Jon ed. *Critical Thoeries: From Lacan To Said*, 'Jean Francois Lyotard', Simon Tormey, pp. 152-167.

Wikipedia. 'White on White'. https://en.wikipedia.org/wiki/White_on_White

4

Silence, Shame and Narrative Agency: A Reading of Tito Mukhopadhyay's *Beyond the Silence: My Life, the World and Autism*

— ***Shibashish Purkayastha***

My purpose in this paper shall be twofold: firstly, I intend to show how Tito Mukhopadhyay in his autobiography *Beyond the Silence: My Life, the World and Autism* explores the tropes of silence and shame that have been central to his experiences of living with a cognitively disabling condition. Secondly, I seek to purport that, Mukhopadhyay's fleeting memory, his apparently disjointed and elliptical narration enables us to re-envision the form of the autobiographical narrative as a genre itself. The increased interest in the issues of disability and impairment has led to a proliferation of autobiographies, memoirs and novels which describe the materiality of living with a [physically] disabling condition. Scholars of literature, film studies and cultural studies have mostly concentrated on aspects of physical disability while certain disabilities resulting from cognitive impairments went unattended. Interestingly, though, there has been a significant development in the field of criticism in exploring issues of cognitive disabilities.

And, as Stuart Murray rightly observes that, "the often hidden nature of cognitive impairment is, possibly, something that even scholars working in the field of disability and cultural narrative, or those utilizing the critical languages of neuro-scientific inquiry, have failed to see" (25). The increased rate of diagnosis (from one in a thousands in the 1970s to one in one hundred today) has precisely led to this narrative fascination with the autistic individual and its reproduction across different media.

Disability Life Writing have served the purpose of acting as "counter discourses" to dominant medical and social understandings of disability. They tend to challenge a tangle of oppressive ideologies and destabilize any claim to a normative or fixed center. Moreover, rather than eliding the body, these narratives insist that critical theory, perception, and subjectivity are all grounded in the "poetics and politics" of the lived and situated body. What we see in disability life writing is a "conscious rendering of altered physicality in prose" (Couser 150). As such, disability life writing offers a necessary "return to the visceral in disability studies," resulting in theorizing that is at once personal, social, political, and embodied. These writers had also posited their critiques against the usage of terms such as deficit, disorder and impairment while describing the condition. Experience of, identity with, and access to the conditions of everyday life are tied up together not only in relation to disability, but in all situations. Drawing on a critical disability study and narrative theory framework, I examine Mukhopadhay's delineation of the tropes of silence and shame that have been central to his experience of living with autism. Tito Mukhopadhyay, in one of his interviews, stated that, coming out as disabled, in the absence of what a culture typical envisions as disability's typical presence, seems a slightly different matter. If an autistic person, for example, is to come out, she or he must actively deny her/his own stance in, as Irving Zola has put it, the "world of the normal". It is the very visibility of normalcy that must be silenced, ignored, denied. It is the person's assumed and apparent stance in the ordinary that makes coming out as, and passing into, disability a different matter for people whose differences do not readily appear to others who unquestioningly assume, and thus "see" only, the structures of normalcy.

Heidi Lourens in her essay "Driving in Unheard Silence: Disability and the Politics of Shutting Up" had suggested that, the politics of silence is crucial to the experience of living with disability. She states that, disability-related silences are mostly created through the confluence of inaccessible physical and social environments and the psychological internalization of these worlds (web). The stigma, shame and silences faced by persons with autism spectrum disorder often tend to exacerbate their health conditions. In different ways and to different degrees, people in many countries view autism as a source of disappointment, annoyance, shame or worse. According to some researchers, stigma may keep the user from seeking diagnosis, from participating fully in their communities. Simply put, stigma influences behavioral patterns of an individual with the condition. The term "autism" was used for the first time by Eugene Bleuler in the beginning of the 20th century. The name originates from the Greek word "autos" (alone) and refers to the psychopathological tendency of turning away from the outside world and focusing on the inner world. Initially, autism was treated as the result of or a part of schizophrenic detachment. The term 'autism' entered the official classification in 1943, when Leo Kanner used it to describe a disorder whose primarily feature was the significant abnormalities of social, cognitive and behavioral function in a few children (APA, 1994; WHO, 2000). My reading of Mukhopadhyay's autobiographical narrative is a move away from the deterministic view of disability and I propose that, Mukhopadhyay's narrative envisions new ways of thinking about bodies and autobiographical narratives. In Mukhopadhyay's autobiographical narrative, he seeks to bring to the forefront the fact that, persons with autism spectrum disorder are not capable of reciprocating feelings in the same way as a person (neurotypical) without the condition. He further mentions that, autism does often affect an individual's ability to understand unspoken interpersonal communication, so someone with autism might not detect sadness based solely on one's body language or sarcasm in one's tone of voice. But, when emotions are communicated more directly, people with autism are much more likely to feel empathy and compassion for others.

Tito Rajarshi Mukhopadhyay was diagnosed with 'severe autism' when he was three. He was brought up in Bangalore and Mysore. He moved to U.S, with his mother, at thirteen. By then, Tito Mukhopadhyay had become a sensation in the autistic community who was bent on defying and disrupting conventional biomedical understandings of the condition. *Beyond the Silence: My Life, the World and Autism* was published when he was twelve. In Mukhopadhyay's narrative, the notion of silence is linked with the lack of or with inadequate verbal competences resulting in disturbances in the exchange of information with the environment. Presumably, language does not serve the autistics as a means of communication, thus in their analysis of the role of silence in reference to verbal communication is out of question. As Anna Bieniarz in her essay "Loneliness and Silence in Autism - Implications for Psychotherapy" notes: Silence in autism may appear in different degrees. The highest degree of silence is manifested in mutism and is interpreted as complete silence, creating a barrier separating autistics from the competent speech users. The silence surrounding autistics possesses the greatest therapeutic value; it reduces the number of stimuli from the outside environment. In these cases silence serves as a defense mechanism, protecting the unformed intra-psychic space from the chaos, and disarray challenging with the disintegration of the personality (web). In the Foreword to Tito Mukhopadhayay's autobiography, Lora Wing states that, before Tito's arrival at the Centre for Social and Communication Disorders, Tito had exhibited behaviors that was beyond the pulpit of commonsensical understandings of autism. It was believed that persons with autism have one or more talents far ahead of their abilities such as talents involving "visuo-spatial or rote memory skills such as calendar calculations, numbers, drawing remembering train time tables and so on. But Tito was apparently able to use long words in complex sentences and to express philosophical thoughts about life" (1). Tito's remarkable ability lay in his ability to communicate using an alphabet board from the age of six years. With the aid of his mother, he wrote down the alphabets on a piece of paper. He was able to respond to the queries by pointing to the letters on the alphabet board to spell his replies. From very early on in his life, Mukhopadhyay showed clear signs of good cognitive ability through his recognition of and the ability to match numbers, letters and shapes. His exceptional abilities points to a certain "narrative appeal" that Stuart Murray referred to in his essay on autism narrative. The narrative appeal of an "autie-biography" is the ability of a text to "exhibit a certain form of personal otherness" (28). Indeed, it is the personification of difference and otherness: a person, just like you or me (so the argument runs), who is in fact nothing like you or me, but "rather subject to a condition that supposedly defies logic and understanding" (38). In the opening section of his autobiography titled "The Voice of Silence", Tito states that, people would often be embarrassed or worried by his actions and doctors would use different terminologies to describe his condition, much to his dismay. Throughout his autobiography, Tito describes his relationship with his mother by bringing in an analogy of the hand and its shadow. It was his mother's lap, which had the "warmth and readiness" which made him socialize, despite his many attempts of withdrawing into himself. He describes instances when he was burdened with a chronic sense of sense of shame.

Mukhopadhyay attempts to re-construct a 'self' after the disruption of the coherence of the self, post diagnosis which is at variance with essentialized biomedical normativizations. In many of Tito Mukhopadhyay's autobiographical sketches, the reader is made aware of the fact that, autism affects not only his view of the world but also his poetic impulses. Tito's sensory perception is clearly modified by his condition. Since he is unable to connect simultaneous sense experiences, he often focuses on his auditory sense, which he considers more powerful than his vision (112).

Besides, Tito has "partial synesthesia" (184) which is why he often perceives sounds or emotions as color (157). Tito's "fragmented sensory experience" (212) inhibits him from forming a coherent understanding of the world. Tito frequently experiences a sensation of losing his body. Sometimes, he describes himself as a disembodied being; at other times, his body seems to be scattered and incontrollable. In his autobiography, Tito mainly talks about himself in the third person, he reports that "[t]he boy refused to accept the existence of his body, and imagined himself to be a spirit" (19). As a result of his virtual being, he "was losing control over his body. A sense of denying its existence was so strong that he could not respond to any situation the way it should have been done" (22). In his autobiography, each chapter addresses an aspect of his mental experience, beginning with his childhood in Mysore and Bangalore, and moving through adolescence in Los Angeles and Austin, Texas. The brain is the central thread to his stories. Through Tito's autobiographical narrative, we are also provided snippets of his family and his relationship with his grandparents, and this becomes crucial to understanding how, at times, they helped him to overcome the stigma, silences and shame that surrounded his condition. He also mentions how memories of having lived with them helped Tito to construct a narrative from the shards of his fragmentary memory. Tito describes how his family looked down upon his mother for her abiding interest in reading. As he states, "she was bad, as the relatives thought that married women who were mothers should not study, neglecting their children. In a country where death is worshipped, where sacrifice is worshipped, where ambition is considered to be the key to greed and vice, she was bad" (7). He also describes his funny relationship with the staircase, which at an early age, he believed that, it would lead to God. Tito recounts an incidents at the doctors' chambers where he had pushed and pulled his parents towards the staircase, much to the wonder of the people around, leading the doctors to conclude that Tito had celebral palsy. Then, he goes on to describe his recurrent dream in which he is accompanied by a gentleman, who followed him everywhere. After a point, he lost contact with all these images that formed around him. In the early years of his life, upon discovering Tito's condition, people had suggested that the boy be taken to a nearby temple which had a healing aura around it. Since, only a miracle could cure him.

In his essay "Autism and Culture," Joseph Strauss proposes a biocultural model of autism in which he suggests that, as an identity group, autism is somewhat amorphous, inclusive, and heterogenous. In current thinking, autism lies along a spectrum, a neat linear progression from "low functioning" to "high functioning." Given the increasing size and diversity of the population classified as autistic, however, it might be better to think of it as an agglomeration, a network of overlapping subgroups, and with the group as a whole defined by boundaries that are notably permeable and porous. Within individuals, symptoms of this condition may significantly vary. Mukhopadhyay, at a certain point in his narratives writes: "Instead of thinking of autism as a disease, with apprehensible cause, a determinate diagnosis, and a possible cure, it might be more productive to think of it as a "disease entity," which, "allows us to move away from the positivist kind of descriptive categories of disease and to think of diseases not as discrete objects but as ranges of bodily differences and reaction" (22). This is what Strauss meant by a "biocultural model of autism", one that discusses illness and disease as emerging from a complex interaction of biology and culture. Eric L. Santner explores the idea of "narrative fetishism" in his essay "History Beyond the Pleasure Principle" where he defines it as, "the construction and deployment of a narrative consciously or unconsciously designed to expunge the traces of the trauma or loss that called the narrative into being in the first place" (14). So narratives, when fetishized, can become a way of shutting our ears to what hurts and scares us the most, a way of not merely narrativizing our silences, but also ridding oneself of the shame resulting from the social ostracization and vilification. Much of the verbal narration or gestured narration was the byproduct of much of the social vilifications. In his narrative, Tito, at certain instances, withdrew into his mother's lap because of the social ostracization.

In his narrative, Tito describes his experience of learning to ride a cycle and his presence in a social gathering would lead to giggles. As he utters in one of the sections in the narrative, People, people all around Not a one to match, I search for a someone But I am a clown to watch! (13)

Tito's deviant embodiment enabled him to remember things and events by associations. After the death of Tito's grandfather, he would forcibly climb up to the bed where the corpse of the deceased was kept. Upon seeing that, the incense sticks were being lighted around the bed, the boy thought they were worshipping the corpse, and it led him to draw the association of the staircase that he believed, led to God. He concluded that, what remarkable things death could do to a person. And, then he decided to work for it. After the death of his grandfather, Tito considered himself to be a spirit without the existence of a body. Narratives such as these, are important in underscoring how people on the autism spectrum command their own storylines. Here, with the aid of the white board and his mother, Tito was able to narrativize his own experiences.

The narrator mentions that, Tito's mother finds interesting rewards for her son's endeavors. For instance, she shoots a picture of him at the end of each day. The prospect of seeing himself in a photograph is highly motivating for Tito, most likely because it provides him with an image of his whole and un-scattered body (151). Not only physical but also cognitive improvements are visually (re)constructed. Tito is well aware that his brain is plastic and adaptive as long as he makes an effort to change its circuits:

> With every new skill I learn, more areas of my brain are exercised. [...] Mother would come home and draw diagrams to show me what my nerves were doing when I struggled with taking down dictated words. On the first few days, she would draw the dendrites and make a chain of them. She would draw them very lightly to show a feeble connection among them. As days passed, she would show a darker connection

> between them because they were supposed to be gaining in strength as I practiced. I could imagine the neurons making a pathway in my brain, as I showed more motivation and less resistance. (171)

Here, Tito refers to the relatively recent scientific discovery that the brain is malleable and adaptive not only in infancy but in adulthood as well. New findings in the field of neuroplasticity, the ability of the brain to reorganize itself as a result of experience, have led to significant breakthroughs in the treatment of autism. The narrative mentions an imaginary conversation between the autistic boy and the child psychiatrist, in which, after the psychiatrist diagnoses the body of having "autism", the boy is seen to further withdraw into himself. As the narrator tells us, the boy was losing control over his body. The sense of denial was so strong that he could not respond to the situation the way it should have done. The narrator also describes the boy's engagement with different activities that involves the use of one's cognitive abilities like solving jigsaw puzzles and crosswords. As the boy felt his cognitive abilities were on par with everyone else, he felt that his body was scattered and it was difficult to collect it together. Such narratives can enable the productive interaction of the voices of the writers in ways that can attempt to empower rather than exploit the disabled subject. At one instance, in his autobiography, Tito recounts:

> "Now that I knew I was autistic, I began to group things under it. I made up a whole list of things that I thought had autism. The curtains that moved in the wind, the big and small leaves that moved a little more with the air because of their suspended positions, the little bits of paper, or the pages of an open book under a fan were classified as autistic. They were affected with autism because they flapped, because they would not respond to any blocks, because they did not talk, and I was sure that they would not be able to imitate the clinical psychologist". (28)

Through the course of Tito's witty subversion, autism becomes less a signifier of pathology than a term for his sense of "extreme connection" or animistic empathy, a term that re-orders the world, dismantling the privilege that attends to the neurotypicals.

Through Tito' narrativization of his experiences, Mukhopadhayay has tried to expunge the traces of trauma, shame and silences that surround his condition, while also demonstrate the capacity of life narratives to facilitate the relational interaction between writers in the negotiation of understandings of disability. Though, the text begins by focusing on the limitations of life with autism, it develops into a collaboration which helps both writers move toward new ways of understanding disability and their own and one another's life stories. Through these narratives, people living with such a disabling condition, are revealed as fellow humans, albeit those with a fundamentally different way of understanding the world. Writers like Mukhopadhyay emphasizes on the need to exorcise some of the myths associated with such a health condition, and as Mukhopadhyay's narratives show, autie-biography can indeed be a valid testament of a person living with autism. Disability narratives, through their unique portrayal of certain experiential vantage points, may be able to move the reader, promote self-reflection, and challenge preconceived notions on disability. Finally, they may communicate the idea that pity is not an adequate emotional response to disability, leading the reader to recognize people with disabilities as a distinctive social group that demands specific social rights. As such, these narratives lead readers to discover an alternative way to see and perceive the disabled person, behind the stories. Thus, while we are keenly aware that these narrative acts and readings are in no way a sufficient ground for social change, they can be perceived at least as a necessary ground (Schaffer and Smith 226).

Works Cited

Bieniarz, Anna. "Loneliness and Silence in Autism- Implications for Psychotherapy". https://www.intechopen.com/books/autism-a-neurodevelopmental-journey-from-genes- to-behaviour/loneliness-and-silence-in-autism-implications-for-psychotherapy. Web 30 18 September, 2019.

Couser, G.Thomas. *Body Language: Narrating Illness and disability. (Life Writing).* New York: Routledge, 2017. Print.

Lourens, Heidi. "Driving in unheard silence: Disability and the politics of shutting up". Journal of Health Psychology. SAGE Journals. 22 April, 2016. https://journals.sagepub.com/doi/abs/10.1177/1359105316643856. Web. 30 September, 2019.

Mukhopadhyay, Tito. Beyond the silence: My Life, the world and autism. UK: National Autistic Society, 2000. Print.

Murray, Stuart. Autism (The Routledge Series Integrating Science and Culture). New York: Routledge, 2011. Print.

Santner, Eric L. "History beyond the Pleasure Principle: Some Thoughts on the Representation of Trauma." Probing the Limits of Representation: Nazism and the "final Solution, vol. 144, 1992.

Schaffer, Kay, and Sidonie Smith. Human Rights and Narrated Lives: The Ethics of Recognition. New York: Palgrave Macmillan, 2004. Print.

Strauss, Joseph. "Autism and Culture." The Disability Studies Reader, ed. Lennard J. Davis. New York: Routledge, 2013. Print.

Part - V

Silence and Resistance; and/as Punishment

1

Political Aesthetics of Silence in Marguerite Duras's *The War: A Memoir*

—*Swarnika Ahuja*

Increasingly Trauma Studies have gained impetus in the past decade and literary narratives arising out of conflict and warring states have become the focus of critical enquiry. *Modernist Women Writers and War: Trauma and the Female Body in Djuna Barnes, H.D., and Gertrude Stein* has focused on how major modernist women writers and their narrative strategies can be read as offering both a feminist as well as an anti-war critique. This paper will attempt to analyse the works of Marguerite Duras and how her works provide an anti-war stance from her position as a woman; the literary techniques she employs to unravel the ways in which she witnessed the war and the predominant role of silence in her archive. Further, in the light of her account, it will also try and assess the scope of the 'memoir/life-writing' genre within Trauma Studies itself

In the lieu of a theoretical basis, Peter Nicholls' essay 'Wars I Have Seen' makes a very interesting intervention in terms of seeing war that will give a crucial perspective on the kind of narrative strategies Duras employs in her work *The War: A Memoir*. In her own words, Duras states how she had completely forgotten writing this diary in the first place, how alien the language seemed to her on finding it years later, how she was forced to confront a " tremendous chaos of thought and feeling" that she couldn't grasp in retrospect.

> How could I have written this thing I still can't put a name to, and that appals me when I reread it? And how could I have left it lying for years in a house in the country that's regularly flooded in winter? (4)

Her account emerges at a crucial juncture in terms of the Second World War. For her diary is focalised from her position as a woman, a wife who awaits the return of her husband while she stays with her lover D. Her diary records the aftermath of the Second World War, the turbulence of the last few days of Hitler's Reich in Paris. Her unique position as a woman, a writer, simultaneously also part of the Resistance network, offers an utterly different account of the war itself- a perspective, a way of seeing war that is often lost in the hullabaloo of heroes returning, and masculine jingoist narratives celebrating bravery and glory.

In various ways, Nicholls tries to formulate the relationship between war and seeing when he postulates the question 'How and from where do we see a war?'(16). He mobilises various metaphors for war itself such as a theatre, a spectacle that we see. War itself employs certain ways of seeing on the battlefield; makes a certain way of seeing more profitable which is dehumanising and violent precisely because it is myopic in some sense. In the sense, the proponents of war cannot see or recognize the other as anything beyond an object to be annihilated completely.

Through these multiple articulations of seeing, he tries to formulate a way of seeing that can be rescued from the totalitarian logic and confinement of war-speak, which is evoked in a spatial sense as much as in a linguistic sense. Thus, seeing becomes literally as a special kind of gaze that penetrates through the 'fog of war' (14), that linguistically and spatially looks beyond the confinement of the battlefield as well as the jargon of war. These ideas come together in his exploration of the example of Gertude Stein, where the act of 'seeing' is sceptic both of the personal 'spectatorial attitudes' (16) as well as the 'we' that presupposes and sees on behalf of the whole nation. While it is true as Nicholls himself admits that to see a war or rather to see anything, some level of distance is required (16); in Stein's case, seeing becomes an act that unfolds the experience of war in a more authentic way that does not come after but through it (17); one that nevertheless does not fail to account her role as that of a woman.

> In Stein's case though the seeing is being done by someone apparently immersed in domestic routine – "Yesterday," she says, " I went my usual twelve kilometres to get some bread and cake" (p.137) - but someone who is also able to reflect on [...] the unreality of wartime existence, with quirky observations undermining conventional wisdoms [...] (16-17).

This example lays bare, Nicholls's own political bias in the sense, that while he is anti-war in his stance, he is sceptic of individual post-war accounts and senses a danger in them, of being guilty of the same kind of myopia accorded to the 'we' that is totalitarian and confining. Between these two dangers, he places this idea of see-ing that is continuous, a constant unfolding through poetic language itself. Here, he is clearly influenced by Heidegger because only in recognising the ability to see through poetry, without putting a full stop at the end but in letting it continually unfold can we rescue this notion of seeing from the homogenising and totalitarian discourse of war-speak.

Only in the state of constant unfolding and unfurling can this act of seeing be truly saved from being appropriated by the same forces it seeks to defy. And this can happen only though seeing in certain ways where seeing itself begins something akin to a specific kind of poetry. That is opposed to the fascist dreaming of Pound's poetry which can only see by 'conflating totality and design' (21), as some kind of blind faith in the 'enormous dream of the fascist state' (21) so to speak. Hence, he is sceptic of the visionary kind of poetics, that ends up being confined by another, different and perhaps more dangerous kind of totality. Against this, he posits for a way of seeing that is more empathetic in a certain sense. This is the notion of seeing he is trying to get at while quoting liberally from Duncan and Oppen, where seeing through poetry is an act of destabilising the order of hierarchy and authority, that breaks through prescribed tunnels of vision itself. It dares to look beyond the deterministic annihilation of the self and /or the other and in its stead places a notion of looking against pre-given orders. That sees, even in a single moment, one's own self as more than a killing warring machine, as an escape from this linguistic and spatial claustrophobia and recognises the self as part of a community. In Duras's case, this self is also gendered.

> I argue for the critical consideration and validation of war writing by women, writing that does not always treat battles and refuses to foreground masculine attitudes toward war and women. Rather, Djuna Barnes, H.D., and Gertrude Stein counter patriarchal or traditional war narratives by featuring women as significant characters who suffer from war and protest it in their literary works. These writers create new narratives that cast war as destructive, perverse, traumatic, and quotidian. By recognizing women writers who write about marginalized aspects of war experience—namely, the experience of living on the home front economy in wartime, as war writers—we can likewise recognize a broader perspective on war experience and work toward a more accurate definition of war writing, one that takes into account women's responses to war and women's suffering (Goodspeed-Chadwick 1).

This notion of suffering that Goodspeed- Chadwick discusses, is largely absent in the dominant war accounts presented by soldiers. This is not so for all writing produced by men but like Nicholls warns that all voices emerging post the war experience need to be read through a certain kind of scepticism, to ensure it does not end up using the same kind of language of war it seeks to oppose. What is often missing from this rhetoric of witnessing war is the suffering, the vulnerability, the grief and the dehumanising effect that war has.

Duras's diary is a significant intervention at this point because as opposed to Broyles she articulates the war completely differently. Her language is one that in no way glorified or grand or sentimental. It is so spare and stripped bare of emotion that it is a language that comes closest to capturing the war experience. Cynthia Cruz in her "Notes Toward a New Language: Holes: On Margueirte Duras" says,

> Marguerite Duras's writing is filled with holes. Her writing is made of holes, filled with holes, because her life is made up of holes. Pock-marked and moth-bitten, it is a map of the disaster.
>
> The writing has holes in it for breath, for breathing, for grasping in the dark for the proper word to describe the precise abject poverty, the exact place in which the writer loses herself, where she becomes lost. It is in the ellipses, in the pause, in the constant caesura, the cut, the comma and stops made by punctuation and also by space on the page.
>
> In *No More*, Duras' final book, a meditation on the end of her life and her imminent death, she writes in tiny marks, like an animal clawing at the gates of death. Less than vignettes, fractured fractures, she leaves the page bare for all of the unsaid:
>
> *Holy Saturday*
>
> What I am going to turn into.
>
> I am afraid.
>
> Come. Come with me.
>
> *Later, the same afternoon*
>
> Let's go see the horror, death (43).
>
> Standing at the precipice, she has no words to describe the wound that is her past. And so the only proper language, the only true means of representing the ruin, the remains, is silence or a kind of silence.

And ironically, it is only by using language so sparingly that she is able to convey the depths of suffering and horror it holds. It is clearly evident in the way she constructs her sentences in her War memoir. They are short, disjointed, abrupt and devoid of feeling and characterised by a physical tiredness caused by warfare that it is at the very limit of language itself.

> It's a red evening. The end of the world. My death's not directed against anyone. Just a simple death. I shall merely have died. It's a matter of indifference to, the moment when I die is a matter indifference to me (8).

What is also missing is this false sense of bravery and strength that is sung and openly celebrated in sentimental war songs, this excess that so often characterise these narratives.

> This evening I think about myself, I've never met a woman more cowardly than I am. I go over in my mind other women who are waiting like me- no one is as cowardly as that [...] Not for a second do I see the need to be brave (22).

This brutal and fearless admission of cowardice is what isolates her further from other women openly expressing grief, weeping lamenting and bravely powering through this period of waiting for the men to return. The breakdown of her psyche is reflected in the breakdown of speech itself. When her husband Robert L. returns, her reaction is one that is at very limit of speech- something bestial, inhuman and incoherent.

> I was shrieking, I remember that. The war emerged in my shrieks. Six years without uttering a cry. I found myself in some neighbours' apartment. They forced me to drink some rum, they poured it into my mouth. Into the shrieks (53-54).

Nicholls discussing Ginsberg's Howl suggests that 'his "howl" is against not only these literal spaces of miserable confinements, but against a closed language which can be broken open only by something as primitive and inchoate as a howl' (13-14).Duras's 'shrieks' then are an attempt to break through from not only the nightmare of war but also the phallocentric language of men; of reason and rationality. Her animalistic shriek tears through the false pretence of a toxic masculine rationality that is also Eurocentric. And she is quick to point this out as well.

> This new face of death [...] has been discovered in Germany–organised, rationalised- [...]. One of the greatest civilised nations in the world, the age –long capital of music, has just systematically murdered eleven million human beings with the utter efficiency of a state industry (49-50).

It is not somewhere else, somewhere uncivilised or barbaric that this carnage has taken place but on European soil, one that is so-called civilised and full of rational, reasonable beings.

What her narrative strategies on the other hand achieve is grant her the opportunity to tend to her grief, her suffering, to inhabit this inconsolable grief where she awaits her husband's return. It is only through writing that she is able to make sense of not only her war experience that would have been otherwise forgotten and suppressed but also allows her to see war in a completely different way, one that is away from guns and tanks and close home. In fact it is only by showing how stress and trauma due to war has spilled into the everyday, domestic spaces that the true horrifying effects of war are conveyed.

> I go into the kitchen and put the potatoes on. I stay there, lean my forehead on the edge of the table, shut my eyes [...] Suddenly it bursts in on me, the obvious: he's been dead for a fortnight. Fourteen days, fourteen nights, abandoned in a ditch (9-10).

It is only in the solitary space as the kitchen that the true reach of the horrors of war are voiced. One where the anxiety of death has trickled into the most banal, ordinary experiences such as preparing a meal.

Duras's narrative opposes the rhetoric of bravery, of patriotism and even chastity for she transgresses sexually by taking a lover in the absence of her husband. And it is only through memory, through language that she is able to challenge and critique not only the war but also patriarchy. It is only through language, no matter how fragmented and infused with silences, that she able to make whole once again the shattered and dehumanised pieces of herself and protest the dominant masculine voices of men.

> One perspective would be to read sequences of catastrophe, survival and supersession as trajectories that recompense the felt depredations to identity; that these works help to reconvene the self. Hal Foster is exactly right to observe that '*In trauma discourse, then, the subject is evacuated and elevated at once*' (Foster 1996. 168). We need to cover both of these movements in the trauma memoir (Luckhurst 119).

This kind of seeing, is therefore also an unseeing of sorts, that rejects mediums such TV that make war a spectacle. That does not let us see war as an event in the past, as already over and therefore needed to be either forgotten or giving rise to the spectacle of public memorialisation. But rather as something that is always lurking in the everyday. It is this kind of seeing that is sensitive, feminine rather than 'grand' and 'visionary' that can humanise the self threatened by war. A way of seeing that can emerge only *through* writing and not *after* it. And ultimately become a testimony of not only survival but also hope. Duras herself is articulating the need for this new language fused with gaps and silences.

> There should be a non-writing, and it will come some day. A simple language without grammar. A form of writing consisting only of words. Words without grammar to sustain them, abandonment as soon as they have been written down (47).

Cruz theorises this as,

> [...] what Duras is describing is a writing made entirely of holes with no connective tissue--the exact replication of her experience. Something shorn of decoration, a writing that turns our gaze to the world and away from the writer. A language

loose and broken, like beads jeweled along a frayed string of thread. Duras's words are symbols, they are images. They escape syntax and grammar. Each word is its own universe of meaning. Each word an image compressed with its own world of meaning, floating on the page. Her words do not attempt to explain, how can they? There are no answers to the brutality she has seen, she has, herself, experienced.

It is only by employing a moth-bitten language, does the experience of War gets articulated at the level of language, one when even animalistic shrieks fail to express, it is the very silence that takes place of what occurred.

To conclude, silence is then not merely an aesthetic category but a political tool in Duras's memoir that resists the filling of these gaps, but rather dramatizes bodily wounds inflicted by the war experience through the wound of language itself.

Works Cited

Broyles Jr., William. 'Why Men Love War'. *The Vietnam Reader.* Edited by Walter H. Capps, Psychology Press, 1991.

Cruz, Cynthia.'Notes Towards a New Language: Holes: On Margueirte Duras', poetryfoundaton.org, 22nd April 2015, https://www.poetryfoundation.org/harriet/2015/04/notes-toward-a-new-language-holes-on-marguerite-duras [Accessed 12th November 2019]

Duras, Marguerite. *The War: A Memoir.* Translated from the French by Barbara Bray, Pantheon Books, 1986.

Goodspeed-Chadwick, Julie. *Modernist Women Writers and War: Trauma and the Female Body in Djuna Barnes, H.D., and Gertrude Stein,* LSU Press, 2011.

Luckhurst, Robert. 'My so-called life: the memoir boom'. *The Trauma Question,* Routledge, 2013.

Nicholls, Peter. 'Wars I Have Seen'. *A Concise Companion to Twentieth-Century American Poetry,* John Wiley & Sons, 2008.

2

Identity Politics and the Re-evaluation of History in the Poetry of Rita Dove and Jean "Binta" Breeze

— *Sukanta Roy*

Personal and collective memory along with social engagement in different conditions creates an existential consciousness which may constitute but not all-inclusive of the conception of identity. History, while being written by the winners and having no such effective tool to distinguish between facts and propaganda, social views, as well as theories, often misjudge and misinterpret incidents leading to oppression and injustice. Emphasising on human endeavours of creativity and aestheticism Rita Dove analyses the mainstream narrative only to deconstruct it and later recreating a new way of perceiving history from personal experience and personal interpretation of that experience. On the other hand, Jean "Binta" Breeze engages herself with the present socio-historical condition of how the western civilisation is implementing more subtle but effective versions of colonialism in terms of international economic policies in the present age by her poetic performances named as 'dub' poetry. Both the poets wanted to re-evaluate the normative perceptions about chronological history in two different ways but their aim was pretty similar: to find out the false assumptions in normative history, to find out possible alternatives in perceptions, to project and promote the multiple views to value the alternative equally, and above all to find a worthy space in that 'history' which previously was controlled by a certain group in power.

While Dove works more with chronological history Breeze works with immediate history which means events that were very directly affecting to the people concerned; for example, for Dove the memory of slavery, plantation, Southern culture, the migration from the South to the North, the Racial prejudices hampering the common life and so on take frequent subjects of discussion, whereas Breeze used to talk more about how the concept of the 'Caribbeanness' in the Caribbean Islands was changing because of stereotyped imaginations about it and how the modern economic conditions such as globalisation, international deals, instead of benefitting the country actually making poorer. It is interesting how many things from the past were ignored and a selective approach to history had been normalised. To begin with history and its double standard selective approach, the concept of 'America' would be a very good subject of study. Normative history had assumed that the European Columbus had 'discovered' America while trying to find India and thus the Caribbean islands were even named as West Indies. The nuances of the terminology 'discovery' speak for the authority of the white Europeans over the rest of the world, even though he had been ill and actually found by the native islanders, therefore, in reality, ignoring the fact that it was the islanders who 'discovered' Columbus and not the vice versa. This European consciousness of 'discovering' or knowing the Caribbean provided an undue privilege and justification to rule them. This European white supremacy became more complex when they started to bring slaves from Africa and slaves were not even considered as proper human beings. J. M Cohen's "Introduction" to *The Four Voyages of Christopher Columbus* talked about the material interest of Columbus as well as interest of enslaving people for their own benefit while visiting the island. However, the entire European supremacy has been criticised by Professor Evan Van Sertima in his *They Came Before Us: The African Presence in Ancient America.* He claims that even in one of Columbus's writing there was a hint that Africans were already present before Columbus and therefore, technically they 'discovered' the Caribbean Islands before Europeans did. About African presence in the New World he gave several examples like the discovery of 'Negroid stone heads' "among the Olmecs and in other parts of Mexico and Central America... .from as early as 800 to 700 B.C. (Sertima 26)", the body features among many Mexicans as having "vivid lips, darken skin, wide nostrils (Sertima 27)" and so on. Though many historians rejected Berry Fell's hypothesis in *America B.C.: Ancient Settlers in the New World* (1978), yet it had a great impact on the imagination of African presence in America as Mi'kmaq hieroglyphs found in Mexico had several similarities with Egyptian hieroglyphs. All these theories though not 'proved' yet tell that there is a possibility that what we know as given history may not be as concrete as we thought. It could be also possible that those hypothetical claims are actually true and the mainstream is not ready to accept them yet and that is why the rejection is supreme. These arguments want to establish that perspectives and views should be multiple and people must be adaptive enough to accept all the possibilities to overcome racial as well as other prejudices.

While arguments can be made to support alternative history, Rita Dove introduces personal intervention and more engagement with the given normative history, only to look into the different perspectives and multiple possibilities in the events because ultimately facts are views told by people and when it is done it is nothing but narratives. The distinctive zone between fact and fiction is blurry and Dove fictionalises those various historical events through her personal experiences to create her art. Thus her poetic sequence *Thomas and Beulah* recapitulates multiplicity from the grassroots level and thus promoting plurality and giving a chance to fill in the wrongdoings of the past or the past social aporias. For her, the consciousness of being able to see through complex issues of social injustice is the way to prevent future social aporias. Thomas and Beulah both are fictional characters based on Dove's real-life grandfather and grandmother respectively. It shows socio-political, as well as emotional condition of people and society through fiction. By narrating their lives not through official history but through personal experience, definitely, it brings an engagement, a sense of belonging and a sense of ownership. In *Thomas and Beulah,* the story itself is divided into two parts; "Mandolin" and "Canary in Bloom", narrating almost the same events from two different people's perspective. Thomas's friend Lem owned a mandolin and in a silly bet with Thomas jumped into the water of a deadly sinking island and died. Thomas received the Mandolin as a souvenir to remind him of the death and the never-ending guilt feeling.

In a documentary, Rita Dove said, "Like a Mandolin Thomas's life reverberates with double meanings, sensuous and lively, gleeful and melancholy at the same time (YouTube)." Here duality is not something to be ashamed of or which may lead to uncertainty but rather something which makes a person human being. This is the mantra of reality of simple life that people make mistakes and guilt feelings are as crucial part of life as the sense of achievement in any sphere. As life is full of love, hate, kindness, selfishness, mistakes and compensation to that mistake, the poem sequence, *Thomas and Beulah* mirrors life itself. Life is never perfect but understanding of that imperfection makes life perfect. Thomas, Beulah or Lem, nobody has heroic ability yet for the close and near ones those mundane common people are important. This is why Thomas always carried the guilt-feeling and the Mandolin, and this is why Dove took the initiative to write the poem sequence on her grandfather and grandmother who are pretty common people. Here values to define greatness or heroism are different than in the movies or literary pieces. It definitely contradicts the established ideologies and institutions by emphasising marginal people and the stories of their lives. In a sarcastic tone it can be said that being a black person to survive in America avoiding murder, lynching and conspiracies is no less a heroic act. Dove's approach to history of the common people with common events in life makes this alternative perspective as people's history. Furthermore, she finds those events worthy enough to create art, which indicates her belief that art is everywhere one only needs to find it out.

"The Zeppelin Factory" is a kind of poem which tells the story of factory workers mainly African American who were almost considered as non-existent and whose values of life was the least concerning thing to the white authority. The poem shows how irresponsible and careless a society can be to treat a human being as nothing. It says that some workers were on the ship when it started to fly possibly by mistake or deliberately to experiment and thereby killing some labourers and letting another one committing suicide. Dove captures the tragic tension of the workers. However, in reality, nobody would care by describing the incident as "muscles and adrenalin/ failing, fell/ clawing/ six hundred feet (Dove 126)". "The Akron" airship where the mishap happened, in bookish history, had no place for regret nor did they recognise such incident. Furthermore, the glorious ship was almost a symbol of US power because according to the official recorded history, UK and Germany had ships run by hydrogen where risks were more and benefits were less, whereas US-made ship run by helium definitely was a technical victory benefitting the army. Dove does not merely introduce the alternative history but also the emotions, its effects on people and so on. History should not be just emotionless reports but rather it should talk about common people, talk to common people and above all it should listen to people; which Dove not only preaches but practices in her art.

The poem "Under the Viaduct, 1932" the father teaches his son to be clever so that he can ditch the oppressive system of "kettle of communal soup" (Dove 127) because being black people in America one must learn to keep a balance between "family and the police (127)." The poem echoes the famous African trope of surviving in an adverse situation no matter what often expressed through the story of Brer Rabbit and Brer Fox where the cunning fox tries to outsmart and harm the Rabbit but the Rabbit with sheer patience, wisdom and intelligence successfully comes out of all sorts of traps. This situation is similar to African American condition in society because they need to be extra careful and very patient to survive. Dove praises that quality of courage and patience at the same time criticising the deliberate cruelty of the white people.

"Canary in Bloom" is the second part of *Thomas and Beulah* where Beulah is Dove's grandmother Georgianna. Dove's personalisation of history comes along with criticising the patriarchal normative expectation from a mother, especially a black mother who is always imagined as a family woman to care and nourish her family not thinking about her own condition such as sexuality, desire, aspiration and dream. The poem "Motherhood" tries to tell that it is fine to make mistakes as a mother and it is okay if someone is less skilled to care for her child. At the same time, it also says that a woman can be more than a mother; she can be an artist, a traveller and so on. Dove in this book actually wants to replace the stigmatised image of African American people as uneducated, cruel, dumb, hypersexual or asexual with a diverse, progressive, intelligent yet very common human being.

While Dove is trying to change the image of African American people by addressing the loopholes in the normative chronological history, Jean "Binta" Breeze is trying to focus on the immediate problems of the Caribbean people like economic crisis, international politics, Capitalism and so on because for the poor condition of the Caribbean Islands after Independence in the 1960s most of the problems arise from poverty and harmful politics. Literally the sunny and beautiful scenario of the Caribbean Islands may be attractive for tourism and this tourism industry is definitely one of the major sources of income yet it reduced the country to nothing but a place of photo shooting for the rest of the world. Most of the businesses are owned by a few and that too by the several foreign people, politicians are puppets on the hands of foreign rich businessmen. That is why when the IMF sanctions a loan to the

Caribbeans it is not something to celebrate but a trap from where there is no turning back. The interest for the money would be scary enough to handle and it would gradually eat up the internal economy forcing the country to ask for more loan. By doing so the debt of the country would be impossible to pay and then the rich industrialised Western countries would use their previous so-called 'help' as a manipulative factor to coerce the country to make deal with them which would eventually demolish the backbone of the country. This is why irrespective of having natural resources, minerals and other resources the country remains poor. The poem "Aid Travels with a Bomb" from the book *Third World Girl* echoes the same tone from the poet.

> 400 years
> from the plantation whip
> to the IMF grip
> Aid travels with a bomb (Breeze 136)

It is a sheer cry and frustration of the poet against the exploitation in the name of help because previously they enemy was visible and they knew against whom they were fighting but now the institutionalised robbing and legal tender almost made it impossible to do anything.

Breeze shows another problem of stereotyping the Islands because people used to imagine the islanders as primitive and lacking human quality. The poem "her course" shows how the Caribbean woman "walks/ with images/ of jungle killings (Breeze 14)." Breeze then questions the validity of people's imagination that still prevails in terms of ideas associated with skin colours and then the value judgement associated with those colours. How is Africa associated always with black colour and Europe with white? People's skin colour cannot define the colours of a continent. Furthermore, in this time of globalisation, which on a different field those European countries are using, how can one distinguish colour code of a country and race? Besides, judging one's identity, possibility and existence based on skin colour which again stigmatised according to preconceived notion of continent and socio-economic condition are wrong in so many levels yet people from the so-called developed countries doing so time and again. In the poem "Anthem for Black Britain" the poet claims that "Britain is no longer white/ we claim this land as the land of our birth (Breeze 171)." The concept of purity in terms of colour and identity has been wrongly put into our head for a long time and this poem tells that anyone can be a British and it should not have anything to do with colour. It promotes equality and tries to obliterate any possible intimidating factors in the process of identity creation. National identity cannot be based on physical traits but rather it should come from the sense of belonging. This belongingness should not be deprecating of others means. While finding a sense of belongingness it should not encourage the feeling of hatred. This is where humanity can triumph over petty selfishness.

In terms of alternative history and perspective is concern Breeze's poem "Riddym Ravings" is a wonderful poem which takes a critical jibe at the literary presentation of woman, the Caribbean and the concept of the third world at large. It primarily criticises Charlotte Bronte's *Jane Eyre* (1847) where the "madwoman in the attic" is the Caribbean woman and Rochester is the representative of proud white European man. Jean Rhys in her *Wide Sargasso Sea* (1966) parodied the story and altered the perspective that it is the white man who tortures Bertha and makes her mad. Similarly the poem utters the pain and anxiety of the woman who is confined in an attic of a foreign land where her husband instead of taking care of her and soothing her arranges another marriage with another woman. Instead of romanticising the relationship with Jane, which *Jane Eyre* does, this perspective shows that the same incident is wrong.

The sense of Caribbeanness has been explored and discussed in the poem "Carib" and "caribbean woman" which tell that to seek identity is one of the most common traits of human beings and only love for a place where that person feels home and love for the people with whom that person feel associated with the most can only define his/her belongingness.

Caribbean woman does
rise she son
wid a drumbeat pon im back...
she does rise she daughter
pon a mountain range a breas
bringin de sweets milk
same time she
cookin
washin
ironin (Breeze 93)

The autonomy, power and pride the Caribbean woman has, is unmatched therefore if her husband abandons her she never breaks down but takes the challenge to do things on her own. The poem also hints that she finds her worthiness in that acceptance of challenge which is part of the struggle she has to take to live in the Island. Thus every aspect of identity is hard-earned and when someone feels home that is where home is. Besides, the 'dub' or the performance poetry is meant to reach to more audience through the application of direct and audio-visual method. Performances make the poem more alive and its dramatic pitch, tone makes it more relatable to the audience to reach to the maximum people possible to make them aware.

Caribbean identity neither is not European one nor an African one but rather it is the Caribbean which definitely has borrowed some elements from Europe, Africa and Asia. Eventually, they have assimilated all the bits and pieces of cultural components and developed many more new components to make a new culture of their own. The social 'aporias' or the loopholes are sides which are unjust and full of atrocities which people like Dove and Breeze try to address so that common people become aware of this and take measurements. First of all people must understand who they are and then only they will understand why they are facing all the injustices. In order to so they need to know and understand their history, not the official one but the hidden one which may be available under the mask of stories, folklore, songs, children's plays, or some unnoticed things. They must educate themselves to be brave enough to understand and face the fear of acceptance, the fear of letting the easy one go to welcome the apparent chaos. Identity is never an easy concept. Many traits are intermingled to each other and many things are very hard to understand yet for both African American and African Caribbean their identity are way more complex than others. Being uprooted from Africa where they had very distinct culture and then facing slavery in the New World and being forced to make unities among the previously diverse communities under one umbrella "Africans", then later after Independence or Emancipation the subtle and complex racial, gender-based as well as economical issues, the migration, interracial relations, religious conversions, war and so on had made their lives so diverse that it is impossible to name it. W.E.B. DuBois's double consciousness is definitely there yet one can argue that there are multiple consciousnesses among them and without understanding each one of them describing the community would be very reductive.

What is interesting in the discussion of alternative history is that it encourages more engagements with understanding of events; it judges less strictly in terms of values between fact and fiction; it assesses its effects on real life and not just dry discussion of events; it accepts multiple views as well as multiple traits on a single being. While both African Americans and African Caribbean people understand their root, all the changes in their lives in the New World are also important to know. Identity being a continuous negotiation between situations and consciousnesses both the poets, Rita Dove and Jean "Binta" Breeze try to reach a point of cognisance and understanding of cultural values of both the communities and while these negotiations continue the concept of identity evolves.

Works Cited

"Thomas and Beulah, by Rita Dove." Youtube, uploaded by Forsicht, 12 May 2012, https://youtu.be/7duHFUjieME.

Breeze, Jean "Binta". *The Third World Girl.* Bloodaxe Books, 2011.

Cohen, J. M., editor. The Four Voyages of Christopher Columbus. Penguin. 1969.

Dove, Rita. *Collected Poems 1974-2004.* W.W.Norton & Company, 2016.

Sertima, Ivan Van. *They Came Before Us: The African Presence in Ancient America.* Random House Trade Paperbacks, 2003.

3

(Re)Articulation of Alternate Sexuality: Questioning the 'Natural' and the Discursive Limits of Sex

—*Aratrika Bose*

Biological Determinism as philosophical reasoning legitimizes various forms of subordination as natural and inescapable, because it is based on supposedly natural and therefore, unchangeable factors. Race and Gender are two major areas where the Individual Body and Body of State are in close association with each other. The power of the State over the actual biological being of the human and his lived experience creates the population of a nation. The state's entity, its people are hence regulated through production of power and thereby produced not only as an individual in isolation but as a part of a group, an ideology, a polity. The human life becomes subject to alterations and interruptions in both corporeal and non-corporeal aspects through what Foucault calls the strategic use of such regulatory regimes.

Butler reads sex as a Foucault-ian regulatory ideal in the sense that sex not only functions as normative but also produces the very bodies it governs. Sex works to construct the materiality of the bodies so as to fold it and package it into neatly defined categories. Gender is the cultural aspect of this sex and like sex; gender too works towards consolidating the heterosexual imperative. As Judith Butler argues in *Bodies that Matter*, "gender is in no way a stable identity or locus of agency from which various acts proceed; rather, it is an identity tenuously constituted in time-an identity instituted through a stylized repetition of acts." Here construction itself isn't just a singular act or subject but a series of repetitive acts over a long period of time that has come to replace truth.

Sex isn't a natural pre-occurring aspect but a gradual process of demarcation and re-configuration to control the body. Therefore what informs the body from the very beginning is a construct— material and cultural. The materiality of the body and the imposition of culture and politics on it cannot be imagined without the regulatory norm right from the birth of the human. Therefore sex as a 'natural' aspect of the human, a given precondition that exists before language is a post truth. This is what Simone De Beauvoir implied when she said one is not born a woman but made one. It is to say that what constitutes the truth of the human being from birth is the constant alterations and reconfiguration of the self; identity is in flux in the process of becoming. This foregrounds the double bind of sex itself— in its continued sphere of influence with the changing power structures of the State, its own propagation of a static identity; a fixed sexed self holds no ground. Beauvoir cites in *The Second Sex,* "woman," (and by extension, any gender) is an historical situation rather than a natural fact. In Merleau-Ponty's reflections in *The Phenomenology of Perception* on "the body in its sexual being," he takes issue with such accounts of bodily experience and claims that the body is "an historical idea" rather than "a natural species."

The 'natural' is without value or meaning, its existence is an assumed precondition, already existing before language and culture. The very minute the natural is defined in the realm of language; it loses its naturalness for it takes on value and meaning. This value is impregnated by cultural definitions and social implications.

Therefore not only gender but sex too is a construct whose materiality exists within the realm of language and culture. So we can argue that if gender is a cultural significance that sex assumes then gender is not so much as succeeded by sex or transformed from sex but instead it replaces sex. Therefore sex doesn't acquire social meanings and transform to gender but instead is replaced by social meanings and in essence gender. Sex is offered as a priori to gender and language, is a construction by language pretending to originate before language.

Juliet Mitchel takes a similar stand in "Femininity, Narrative and Psychoanalysis". She argues how the pre-oedipal stage is not isolated as a primal innocence from the symbolic order but instead provides the contrast that lends the castration complex to femininity. The semiotic pre-oedipal, the very notion of heterogeneity exists by law of the symbolic itself. So the two semiotic and symbolic unlike Lacan's stipulation are detached, instead the polyphonic semiotic order exists by the didactic virtue of the symbolic order. Hence the semiotic can never be an alternate to the symbolic in essence, the carnivalseque disruption of language cannot seek to undo the patriarchal phallic aspect of language. Instead the only way to overthrow the binary of the symbolic order is from within the symbolic order itself. Hence for the entire power praxis of language to dismantle the ontological basis of language needs to be questioned and redefined.

In Manju Kapur's *A Married Woman* Astha's first sexual awakening occurs when in an act of lovemaking Aijaz transforms to Reshma. As opposed to earlier, Astha's desires are no longer linked to the body or the incessant need to be physically attractive. Instead she harnesses her mind and intellect. As Astha has redefined what she desires in herself her parameter for sexual arousals also change. Astha's sexual arousal is enhanced by the respect and equal treatment in the eyes of the people she met, be it a boy or a girl. Gender recedes to the background, it is just like the physical beauty or clothes you were, once important now don't matter to her anymore.

Yet, Astha's desires aren't so well defined and putting taglines like bisexuality or lesbianism to it. It would be oversimplification at this point which is why Kapur too is careful not to use these neatly ordered definitions. Instead Astha's exploration of the self is filled with complexities and blurred lines where definitions and orders keep overflowing from their borders. If desire is the untainted raw love we will for another human being, emotions then transform this emotion into the realm of cultural meanings. The social implications then start to get infused with our desires. Instead identities should define roles as individuals should be able to choose the imprints their bodies leave behind but the pedantic order of the society dictates roles based on categories of identities like gender and religion among others and this leaves with fixities and identities that are trapped in stereotypes and post truths.

Agency itself is formed by a social and subject negotiation. Agency cannot be pure, or natural as I keep stressing, untouched by the power praxis of the society that bears heavily on the psyche of the child from the moment it is aware of words and what they mean. Therefore the people are gender phobic are also informed by this very power praxis. Riki Anne had a gender reassignment surgery and identifies not as transsexual or intersex but gender oppressed. David Valentino in "One Percent on the Burn Chart Gender, Genitals, and Hermaphrodites with Attitude" recalls a conversation with Riki Anne where in a workshop s/he invites people to examine her vagina. But even after requesting them to not compare her vagina to others the observers couldn't help but exclaim, "It's just like mine!" Riki states how it was impossible for them to just observe hir vagina as an entity in its own, they had to compare it to their own in order to place it as a coherent idea within the semantic and socio-cultural signifier. Anne exclaims, "People say I transgress the gender system; it is undeniably the case that it is the gender system which transgresses all over me." Anne exists in relational degree to heterosexuality, how similar or different she is to it.

If language gives recognition, and recognition is power then citation of these norms into laws is the main tool of creating marginalities in society. The law of sex and desire is fortified and idealized as the law to the extent of how much it is reiterated by the law and produced by the law. Therefore the State needs to be reconsidered as a series of normative injunctions that materialize and propagate borders and differences. It is important to remember that the criminalization of same-sex activity is no ancient Indian tradition, but a legal provision introduced as late as the nineteenth century by the British colonial government.

The politics of naming and language is thus very important aspect of Gender Movements. Many political groupings have come to prefer the term 'queer' to 'LGBTI' (Lesbian, Gay, Bi-sexual, Transgender, Intersex). The latter term can freeze identity, because, to the original LGBT, Intersex has been added on as a separate identity. The use of queer then, is a deliberate political move, which underscores the fluidity of sexual identity and sexual desire. The term suggests that all kinds of sexual desire and identifications are possible, and all these have socio-cultural and historical co-ordinates.

The attempt is at not only arguing against sex as natural but also problematizing the notion of 'the natural' itself. If heteronormativity is natural and homosexuality is unnatural then on what grounds are natural and unnatural determined? Therefore what is required is a redefinition of what constitutes natural, and whether identity, sexuality and desire can even be natural? At present, a dis-identification with the normative terminologies like sex, gender and natural need to be encouraged. If sex— and its cultural counterpart, gender— is a performance, then it is in this act of performativity that the space for various other sexualities beyond the binary of male female can be recognised.

Andrew Sullivan in *Virtually Normal* finds fault in this entire concept of 'outing' which to him is also relegating to the same heteronormative binary of being either in or out of the closet. It lays emphasis not on the individual but the entire act of coming out, as if it is a vector of absolute change in the individual. That stands in strong contrast against the entire premise of normalising sexual desire. Queer theory, then, neither tries to make claims of notions of lesbian, gay, bisexual, transgender nor does it dismiss it as being of any influence to the identity formation of the individual. Instead, it tries to foreground the intervention of identity politics into the body and mind of the individual. Hence queer theory and gender too, studies sex and sexual desire/orientation beyond the dimensions of social and not biological at all.

In a recent interview with the cast of "Made in Heaven", the recently hit Indian web series by Amazon Prime, Arjun Mathur is asked by the anchor his experience of the depiction of a gay man and going against the usual stereotypes of gay men portrayed by Indian multi-media as effeminate. The anchor's question was well intended, but Jim Sarbh objects the very premise arguing that she reduced the complexities of the character his daily struggles and ambitions all to his sexual orientation. The character depicted is layered struggling with class issues, social mobility yet all that faded in the face of his "masculine gayness" that baffled the anchor so much.

The entry point to this dis-identification must occur with the realisation that gender relations emerge before the emergence of the 'human'. Before the sex of the baby is revealed, the unborn child is loved in an unsexed language, as 'my baby' or 'my child'. But as soon as the sex is revealed the child in being named as he or she enters the gendered discourse. The nursery is painted in a particular colour, the clothes are decided accordingly, all this even before the child can form the self. And with intersex babies, without the proper naming their very humanness comes into question. Therefore gender not only generates the human but against it the inhuman or less human like the queer community. The individual's somatic makeup is delimiting, where the body is supposed to be distinct from the mind but isn't. So therefore a gender and sexual coherence is forced.

In this understanding, the somatic makeup of the body is a distinct amalgamation of the physical, the environmental and the societal. If, owning to technology, human intervention has changed the outside environment then the spatial world has also interceded into the human body. Human bodies grow differently in different parts of the world with respect to diet, staple food, climate and development of technology. Some women are more athletically built than others, some have wider skeletal postures others are naturally leaner. Similarly, in gender-sex distinctions, gender norms influence gender roles from a very young age. And provide delimitations and boundaries to what a young child is pushed to do or expected to achieve. This in turn forms the strength capacity and mentality of the child. When it has crossed a certain age of malleability then the very norms use the differences to categorize the genders.

Santhi Soundarajan was an Asian Games athlete who was disqualified after winning the silver medal because she failed to pass the gender test. Later reports suggested that her upbringing in an impoverished state where she only received proper meals post puberty was a viable factor behind the failed test. According to the Indian game officials she did not possess the characteristics of a woman. Initially introduced in 1966, this test was a perverse parading of the body in front of doctors who just needed long hair, big breasts to agree to their womanhood. This foregrounds the gender traits overwritten on biology.

The genetic, chromosomal and physical reproductive organs aren't all linked to determine male female bodies. In fact there have been many cases of high testosterone in woman even with the XX chromosomes and vagina. Similarly many women have displayed varying chromosomes of XO, which is single X chromosome and XXY or XXX irrespective of a perfectly functional vagina and the right amount of oestrogen. It goes on to show how even individual scientific parameters for determining gender like chromosomal or hormonal are inadequate sometimes to place masculinity and feminity neatly folded within a body.

The female sex is associated with a feminine gender role and behaviour just like man is forced to live up to impossible standards of masculinity, strength and bravery. We millennial have all been familiarised with these gendered behaviour paradigms in every family gathering, to talk softly, sit with knees together and the, saving the best for the last, opt for a job as a teacher because it gives you reasonable timings to manage the home and the job. I realise how these examples might come across as clichés but they are also true, relevant even today. These stylised repetition, performance of gender roles and behaviourisms have culminated in years of gender oppression. Today we see intersex children being forcibly assigned one genital status after consulting physicians on which genital they can alter or cosmetically hide with better ease.

In Arundhati Roy's *Ministry of Utmost Happiness* Anjum an intersex child, who later transforms to a woman, is called a queen without a court, a clown without a circus. Incendiary border runs through her. Being a 'hijra' Anjum is beyond the fixity of language and culture. The anxiety of the world that cannot place her calls her unnatural and pushes her to the periphery. Gender roles govern her; she is forced to dress like a boy and sing in a hoarse voice by a mother who decided that since the penis was larger than the vagina her child must be a tamed into a boy. When her voice starts to break infusing the masculine with the feminine cultural and linguistic constructs cannot cage her and Anjum must embrace her border than struggle to be a part of the centre. A red sari, castrated penis, an adopted child and a guest house over a graveyard gives Anjum an 'anjuman' or 'mehfil' of acceptance. Her world is in the margins and she redefines it as the centre rather than moulding herself to be in the centre.

Counter hegemonic cultural practices must recognize the margin as a site for transformation, as bell hooks says, "...definite distinction between that marginality which is imposed by oppressive structure and that marginality one chooses as site of resistance, as location of radical openness and possibilities". These third spaces, or borderlands, are based on the radical openness and the lack of dogma. It is grounded in the postmodern thought of seeing a conclusion as never being final but instead as a starting point for further exploration. The margin becomes that grey area of endless possibilities, always flexible, vibrant, controversial and moreover radically open.

Identity fixity is often imposing coherence on what heteronormativity sees as chaos. The politics of ontological coherence insists on caging desire and longing outward borders of body and its place in the public spaces of nation. It then calls the pretention and performance as natural, one that it itself imposed. The violence that ensues comes to a full circle. The one particular aspect of a human is forced to stand in for the universal, and the anxiety of such a belief forces society and nation to undulate compositeness to the universal by subjugating the particular. The only way to undermine this ontological need is by foregrounding the idea of non-coherent individualism and particular aspects of the human without distorting the universal. The aim is to escape the tyranny of 'normal' and instead normalise pluralities.

Works Cited

Butler, Judith. *Bodies that Matter*. Roudedge. 1993.

Butler, Judith. "Performative Acts and Gender Constitution: An Essay in Phenomenology and Feminist Theory" Theatre Journal, Vol. 40, pp. 519-531. Johns Hopkins UP. 1988.

Butler, Judith. *Undoing Gender*.Rotledge. 2004.

Harper, Phillip Brian Harper, et all. editor. *Queer Transexions of Race, Nation, and Gender*. Duke UP. 1997.

Kapur, Manju. *A Married Woman*. Penguin India. 2009.

Menon, Madhavi. *Indifference to Difference: On Queer Universalism*. Minnesota UP. 2015.

Menoon, Nibedita. *Seeing Like a Feminist*. Zubaan. 2012.

Roy, Arundhati. *Ministry of Utmost Happiness*. Penguin India. 2017.

Appendix

Seminar Report

Day 1 (October 23rd, 2019)

The first day of the two day UGC Sponsored National seminar on the theme, "Speaking Silence: History, Politics and Psychology"witnessed a footfall of young researchers, scholars, professors and students from all across the country viz Maharashtra, Uttar Pradesh, Karnataka, Rajasthan, Sikkim, Assam, Jharkhand, and Delhi. There were one hundred and thirteen participants along with 39 paper presenters. The topic was well received by the audience attending the seminar. The seminar proceedings are as written below.

Introductory Remarks:

The Seminar began with introductory opening remarks by co-convenor Dr Sucheta Chaturvedi. She asserted on how 'silence' as an idea needed deeper insights which can be provided by revisiting the texts and approaching the same through a multi-disciplinary perspective. She further spoke on concerns about revisionism, a redressal of erasures and gaps in representation is the impetus of underpinnings of postcolonial writings. She then highlights beyond the imperative towards self-representation, there is also the other aspect of recovery—to bring voice, to re-memorialize what has been consigned as silence. She stressed on how the seminar through cinema, philosophy, history, psychology, and politics would delineate the manifestations of silences.

Welcome Address:

The welcome address was delivered by Dr Pratyush Vatsala Tripathi, the Principal of Lakshmibai College and Convenor of the Seminar. With much zeal and zest she addressed the flamboyant audience and instilled in them more vigour and vitality. The chief guest Prof Chandrakala Pudia, the keynote speaker Prof Nandini Sahu, and chair Prof Girishwar Mishra were all introduced to the audience and welcomed by her with mementoes and planters. Afterwards she started her address by merging meaningfully with the topic of the National Seminar. She articulated how silence is familiar to all but very difficult to define silence. She further spoke with a reference to tenth century text Bhamati Tika which speaks of a woman Bhamati who for complete eighteen years only lighted lamp while her husband Vachaspati worked on analysis of a text Brahma Sutra. Touched to see her dedication in silence, he named the book Bhamati Tika. Then she went on describing different types of silences in our daily life and said how silence can even be a weapon. She said Bhishma and Buddha were both silence for different reasons. She also said silence becomes an integral part of Indian Philosophy and spoke how silence was important even for western literary thoughts. She drew references from multiple scholars, literati, and philosophers like, Heidegger, Virginia Woolf, William Wordsworth etc. she reminded the audience about how words go meaningless sometimes and silence gains immense power and meaning there by concluding the address and drawing attention of the audience to different expositions of silence.

Inaugural Address by Professor Chandrakala Padia:

Prof. Padiabegan her address by talking about two aspects of silence—to be silent and to be silenced. She conveyed how difficult is it to maintain silence. She said silence is an energy of social justice. She further reminded how emotions are important to nurture individuals. She said emotions do wonders and when it does there are people who try to suppress the sources of emotions and she went on to say how female emotions are suppressed. She referred to Edward Said and Foucault's idea of power, cultural silence, and identity. She ended her speech by stressing on the need to give voice to the marginal silences.

Keynote Address by Professor Nandini Sahu

Prof Nandini Sahu began her disquisition by drawing attention towards sensitive topics like Dalit Studies, LGBTQ issues, Women studies and few topics under history, politics and postcolonial studies that are silenced. She also spoke of overemphasizing or glamorizing silence which she argues is not required. She journeyed the audience through her poetry collections and works that represented silence and its manifestations. She took the audience through an interesting story of a house cleaner named Sukuma who had facial tattoos imposed by her husband to possess her as his personal entity and how Sukuma bore this silently for years. She said house cleaners like Sukuma are extremely marginalized and needs a voice and academics like her who are more empowered can be voices to them. She urged on bringing partially silenced topics like Folklore to the forefront by positive discourses. She stressed on the idea of organizing seminars and said they are spots were ideas are germinated and thus one must keep the spirit of discussions in seminars. She further talked about two mediums that can rescue one from being silenced. One, being the louder voice, second being a writer writing the unsaid. She also had references fromPlato's Cave theory and Helen Cixous' Laugh of Medusa to delineate the semblances of voice. She concluded her address by giving a clarion call to writers to write about underpinnings of silent voices.

Presidential Address by Professor Girishwar Mishra

The speaker appreciated the audience for their interest to inspect a difficult topic like silence through the medium of this seminar. He emphasized that marginal voices need to be heard and there is a need to give voice to the voiceless margins. He articulated how literature is in a way, speaking silence. He brought to limelight how marginal literature is silent literature and how important it is it to listen to the voice of the margin which further gives voice to their silence. He congratulated the college, efforts of the Principal and Department of English for bringing up such a valid topic which was much needed in the era of chaos. He also spoke of how silence has meanings in different contexts and how important is it to value silence.

Plenary Session I (11:30 am – 1:00 pm)

The theme of first plenary session of the Two Days National Seminar was "Mapping Silence and Its Speech" chaired by Prof Chandrakala Padia (Retd. Prof., Dept of Political Sciences, B.H.U. Varanasi). The panellists were Prof. Girishwar Mishra (Ex Vice- Chancellor, Mahatma Gandhi Antarrashtriya Hindi Vishwa Vidyalaya, Retd. Prof. Psychology), Dr. Nilofer Kaul (Practising Psychoanalyst), and Dr Arjun Ghosh (Associate Professor. IIT Delhi). The discussion began with a talk by Girishwar Mishra on "The Shades and Voices of Silence". The speaker appreciated the audience for their interest to inspect a difficult topic like silence through the seminar. He emphasised that marginal voices need to be heard and there is a need to give voice to the voiceless margins. He said literature is in a way speaking silence. He said silence is a process and a context. He further said no meaning will be communicated if silence is absent. He said rational noise is important for silence to be foregrounded and vice-versa. He discussed two silences he came across. One—Imposed silence. Two—Desirable silence. He also discussed the work 'Roar of silence' by the renowned Hindi poet Ageya. He spoke of necessity of silence to calm the self. He spoke of the importance of yoga, and practising silence to improve life. His paper also emphasised how protests are silenced for political agendas. The paper re-emphasized the importance of silence and positively practising silence. Next, the chair invited Dr. Nilofer Kaul to speak on "Psychoanalysis and Silence: Listening Beyond the Noise of Words to the Music of silence". Dr. Kaul began by drawing attention to the dual process that happens while listening. She said, while listening one also listens to one's own thoughts. She went on tom talk about ruptures and breakages in speech, which further hangs on as dual entities, merging on with continuities of speech. She narrates and re-reads the story of Philomela to decipher silence that is moving towards becoming a voice. She also mentions and interprets the character of 'Joker' in *Batsman* and *Superman* series and retells it from Joker's perspective. She concluded by reminding the audience of the props that silent characters use in-order-to de-silence and voice on. Next, Professor Padia invites Dr Arjun Ghosh to present his paper "Silence in Digital Age". Dr Ghosh spoke of print media and its evolution history in the context of the western world. He talked about how initial times print media rescued events from surveillance. He went on to say how the right to protest is vanishing in the contemporary times. He reminds the audience on how ban on right to protest can affect university education. He asserted on the importance of being critical and thus full of voice. He pointed on 'internet shutdowns' which silences digital reporting. He also spoke of how social networking sites create a collective consciousness about reactions and feelings of the mass and how that can further manipulate and reject the real matter. He concluded by talking about how government manipulates media to fulfil political agendas.

The plenary session ended with Professor Padia's insights and comments on the panel and presenting if her own paper titled "Silence in Politics: Acceptance of Status Quo or Resistance to Status Quo". Prof. Padia elaborated the concept of silence in Politics. She said silence is a response without voice. To ignore silence is to validate silence. She spoke how Derrida's theory of deconstruction helps to construct a perfect idea—silence all the ideas and begin anew. She talked about the book *In the Shadow of Silent Majority* and discussed the idea of silence mentioned there. She critiques the consumerist tendencies and homogeneity of the masses moving towards a fad. She also mentions utilitarianism is when the society is neutral and thus no contrasting voices affecting the peaceful silence. She spoke on how different labour, work and action are. And stressed how important action is as it helps the others around you. She spoke of violent inertia and how it affects the whole system. She concluded by urging the audience in identify violence in the voice and changing it for the good

Plenary Session II (1:45 pm – 3:15 pm)

Professor Jayanti Chattopadhyay, retired Professor at the Department of Modern Indian Languages and Literary Studies, University of Delhi presided over as Chair for the culminating plenary session for the day titled "Creating a Dialogue with Silence" which included presentations from Dr. Sanjay Kumar and Professor Anil Aneja.

The first presentation was made by Dr. Sanjay Kumar, Associate Professor at Hansraj College, University of Delhi, titled "And I Have Said Nothing: Performing Silences". Drawing upon his experiences with Pandies (a theatre group founded by him), Dr. Kumar provided the audience with critical insights and potentialities for the representation and articulations of silences within the fold of activist theatre. Making remarkable use of the work undertaken by his theatre group, he highlighted the therapeutic possibilities of activist theatre to bring forth and process various kinds of trauma, both sociological and political. He illustrated the pragmatic scope of his argument using audio-visual clips of the work undertaken by Pandies; their work with children in Nithari Village in Noida and with the youth of Kashmir.

The second presentation for this session was made by Professor Anil Aneja ofDepartment of English, University of Delhi, titled "Screams of Silence: Intersections Between Disability and Literature". Bringing forth a unique perspective with regards to conversations about silences, Professor Aneja argued for engaging with the silences that surround the politics of disability and its representation. Drawing upon a range of canonical Indian and European texts such as the Mahabharat, Gulliver's Travels, Jane Eyre and Lady Chatterley's Lover,Professor Aneja provided the audience with critical alternative readings of these texts from the viewpoint of the disabled other, often forcefully placed upon the margins of the text (and by extension) and society.

Technical Session

The first day of the conference came to a close with a round of paper presentation by scholars and academicians from diverse disciplines. The presentations were divided into three Panels, outlined hereafter:

Panel One: Mapping Silence through History, Literature and Culture

The first round of paper presentations for the day began with this panel chaired by Dr. Joy L. K. Pachuau, Professor at Centre for Historical Studies in School of Social Sciences, Jawaharlal Nehru University). This session had a total of nine presentations which threw light on various issues and ideas pertaining to silence under different disciplines and themes.

The first presentation by Kuntal Tamang titled, "Denying the Dalit Identity: The Silence of the Kami, Damai, and Saraki Communities of Darjeeling and Sikkim" examined the expressions, or the lack, of the Dalit sensibilities amongst the Kami, Damai, and Saraki communities (the three Scheduled Castes) in Darjeeling and Sikkim and tried to understand whether the self-erasure of the Dalit identity was a result of the overwhelming assimilative nature of the larger Gorkha identity or was a strategy of silence to negotiate a space for itself.

Exploring the use of Silence as a form of resistance in Pakistani art, Antara Bhatia in her paper, "Silence and Estrangement in Post Partition Pakistani Art" examined the paintings of various Pakistani artists post-1947 and the ways in which isolation and silence in their art had become a means of representing the troubled milieu they occupied.

"*Shut up! Vaaya Moodu! Pesadhe*!" (Shut your mouth and do not speak): Imagi(in)ng a Silent Heterocosm in Vaayai Moodi Pesavum

(2014)" was the title of the next presentation by B. Geetha. It emphasised on understanding the metaphor of communication in the film represented through speech and speechlessness and analysed how the breakdown of verbal expression led to the newly invented language of silence and gestural performance.

Anjali Verma in, "Engaging with Wordlessness in Research and With(in) the Researcher" Looked at a peculiar form of Silence in academicians and researchers, who are at a loss of words to express themselves. This writing engaged with the question of whether it was important to open to Silence in academia, giving some meaning to the non-verbal and unarticulated thoughts, which had a capacity for expression, in forms other than words.

The fifth presentation was by Shibani Phukan titled, "The Other Side of Silence: Literature from the North-East" tried to look at literature from the North-East region of the country as an attempt to resist silencing through writing its own narrative and as a necessary approach to avoid homogenising the complexity and diversity that North-East had to offer."

Gaurav Kumar's paper, "Vat Chouboliri" : Reading Narrative/ Resistance in Silence" analysed the dynamics that constituted Chouboli's silence, subjectivity and resistance, and the political contexts constructing the princess as a subaltern figure, a silent object to be won in a conquest, thereby hoping to recover some semblance of a subaltern consciousness in Rajasthani folklore.

Prajakta Simon talked about revisiting the silenced memory and history of the "presence of the past" that had arisen from an anxiety to legitimize the experiences of the 'present.' She necessitated the reading of silences as irony and provocation for enculturation and appropriation of the de-territorialised subjects in her paper "A Studyof Seamus Heaney's *Death of a Naturalist (1966), Door into the Dark (1969),* and *Wintering Out (1972).*

Shalini Shah in "Representation of Nepali Subaltern under Political Disintegration in Manjushree Thapa's 'The Tutor of

History'" discussed history as a portrait of marginalised people under political disintegration, and further to justify that Manjushree Thapa's sympathy with poor and downtrodden, had lend a political edge to her revisionist history which presented the subalterns perspectives, ignored in nationalist, often elite historiography.

The session ended with Sashi Teibor Laloo's paper titled, "The Partition Of 1947: Khasi Lives Mattered Too!" wherein he explored the silent voices of Khasi lives in the North-Eastern region of the country.

Dr. Pachuau, the esteemed chair for the session then provided her critical inputs for all the presenters and talked about mapping silence through silence, history, film and literature. She also provided insight on the psychological, political and contextual silence.

Panel Two: Discursive Engagements with Silence and the Moving Image

Professor Subramaniam Raman Iyer presided over as the Chair for this panel of paper presentations. Introducing each presenter, Professor Iyer made critical remarks with regards to each presentation and concluded the session with his own presentation.

The first presentation for the session was made by Mercy Jill Jill titled, "Untangling 'Her' Silences Women in Select Hindi Films of Twenty First Century". Her paper reads films such as, *Devdas* (2002), *Aakrosh* (2010), *Parched* (2015) etc. in the light of silences the female characters experienced in the contrasting loud circumstances of family ties, patriarchy, caste.

The second presenter, Minakshi Kaushik's paper was titled "The Silence of the Archive: A Historiography of Women Directors in Indian Theatre". Her presentation traced the nature and ideological underpinnings of the silence operating in the documentation of women directors' productions in the archives of The National School of Drama, Sangeet Natak Akademi etc.

Jyoti Singh made the third presentation titled “Disability and Visuality: Video Blogs as ‘Countervisuality’” wherein she explored the convergences between politics of disability and visuality. Using examples from YouTube Channels, she problematised the existing negative constructs associated with physical disability throughout dominant visual culture.

The fourth presentation was made by Shuchi Sharma and Kanika Lakra titled “Revisiting Draupadi: A Critical Study of Saoli Mitra's Five Lords Yet None a Protector”. They analysed the tragic journey of Draupadi, through Saoli Mitra's text to reinterpret and revisit mythological women's experiences from a fresh perspective in terms of form, style and text.

The fifth paper by Ruqayya Bahar was titled “Patriarchal Manipulation of Faith and Silencing of Women in Tehmina Durrani's Blasphemy and Fadia Faqir's My Name is Salma”. She drew upon *Blasphemy* and *My Name is Salma*to uncover how men try to silence women for their own gains; further reflecting upon the need of rising above conventional silence.

The sixth paper titled “Polluted Daughters, Paedophilia, Silence and Memory: A Journey from Adolescence to Womanhood in The Color Purple and What Lies Between Us” was read by Shweta Saroha and Himani Sharma. Their paper examined how paedophilia, silencing and traumatic memories challengestraditional father-daughter alliance and highlights how hegemonic masculine desire has harmful physical and psychological effects on women.

Shweta Sengar made the seventh presentation titled “Exploring Silence as Feminist Strategy: An Indian Perspective on Shashi Deshpande's That Long Silence”. Reading silence as a feminist strategy, her paper examines how Jaya battles authoritarian and male hegemonic discourse and her struggle against the tide of haunting memories and the appalling floods of objects forces her into silence.

A concluding presentation titled “Speaking Silence – Legal and Ethical Perspective” was made by Professore Iyer, in which he examined the consequences of silence threatening the larger interest of the population, in the backdrop of present situation in J & K, United Nations' Peace Keeping Missions etc.

Panel Three: Silence and the Subaltern Consciousness

Dr Vinita Gupta Chaturvedi, Associate Professor at Department of English of Delhi College of Arts and Commerce, University of Delhi directed this session as a chair, which began with her paper titled, "Silence as Passive Resistance: A Reading of Amitav Ghosh's The Hungry Tide" wherein she examined how silence in *The Hungry Tide* tries to articulate the suppressed voice of the peasants in remote Sundarbans; and how silence functioned as a form of passive resistance by the marginalized.

Chandreyi Mukherjee analyzed the complexity of Naoko's silence with reference to her psychological problems and the dangerously widespread social malaise of "Japan- suicide" in her paper titled ""We could face each other over coffee cups in total silence": Analyzing Naoko in Haruki Murakami's Norwegian Wood". It investigated the silence of Naoko as a tool for the predominance of male narration and the justification of male subjective memory.

The objective of the third paper by Priya Dileep was to decipher a melding of unexplored archival documents and ethnographic research, an investigation of linkages between the constructions of Kochi's emerging modernity and the production and dissemination of the idea of regression in "History's Phantom Limb: Re-membering the Devadasis of Kochi".

Reha's paper, "Breaking Silence in Black and Dalit Women Autobiographies" studied the strategies that the subaltern such as black women and Dalit women used to break silence by taking up Lucy Delaney's autobiography *From the Darkness Cometh the Light or Struggle for Freedom* and Faustina Bama's *Karukku*. Black women autobiographers brings to the fore that their gender had been a key cause of their severe treatment in slavery.

"Caste and Class Struggle: Studying the Marginalization of Potters of India" was the title of Sangeeta Jawla's paper in which she looked at the real life artefacts that had been created by the potters and the creation of the narratives that surrounded that material. These oral/textual narratives were compared to the real life narratives gathered through documentation in parts of Rajasthan, Haryana, Tripura, Maharashtra and Tamil Nadu.

The ethnic conflict between the Tamil and the Sinhalese was discussed by Santu Neog in his article, "Ethnic Conflict in Funny Boy" by analysing the subjectivities rooted in history in literature which brought out the different ways Selvadurai had given voices to the silences of history and looked at the redeeming role of history critically.

Swasti Sharma's research paper, "'Dalit Feminists as Public Intellectuals: A Study of Resistance against Patriarchy in the Works of Bama and Meena Kandasamy'" examined the silences in Dalit feminists/public intellectuals. Exploring the survivor's, a focal point of the paper was close textual analysis of the gynocritical approach adopted by contemporary Dalit public intellectuals to repudiate gender performance.

Vandana Lal in her paper titled, "Historical Silencing of the Dalit Consciousness: Understanding the Emphasis on Dalit Theory in The Cracked Mirror" proposed that T\theoretical concepts held the power to intervene the cognitive domains of both the oppressed as well as the oppressor, and could impart unity, continuity, and intensity to experience. She suggested that Dalit theory must emerge and alter the place and position of the Dalit as an outsider in the theoretical realm.

The last presentation of the session was by Dr. Prerana Sinha titled, "Silence in Partition Stories of Manto and Ghosh" where she touched upon transgression and the inevitable dispersion of subjectivity on madness, as viewed by Foucault in his interest in avant-garde art that compelled him to probe the limits of reason that tend to reveal truths that were not rationally accessible.

Dr. Chaturvedi concluded the session by appreciating all the presenters and providing them meaningful and critical feedback with suggestions and questions to ponder upon.

Day 2 (October 24th, 2019)

TECHNICAL SESSIONS

The second day of the conference began with a follow up to the first round of presentations, which were again divided into three Panels based upon their subject matter. A short synopsis of these papers follows herein:

Panel One: Revisiting Silent Self/S: Engagement with Theory and Genre

Professor H.S. Prasad presided over as the Chair for this panel of paper presentations. Listening intently to each presenter's arguments, Professor Prasad closed this panel a short presentation of his own.

Anibal in his paper titled "A Secret Song: Trying to Read Coetzee's Foe" discusses the "epistemological and ethical problems" inherent in tracing the subject positions of racial or gendered 'Others'. In so doing, he looks at certain western literary texts such as Wide Sargasso Sea which exposes the silences that have maintained the fragile fabric of lies that perpetuate the facades of Western civility.

Gagandeep Kaur Ahluwalia in "Echoes of Silence in Time and Being: An Exploration of the Self in Silently Lived Lives" connects the gaps in language and feeling to experiences of being silenced in women's narratives. Reading silence as choice and choice lessness, he reads silence as filling the gaps between feeling and experience, between what is seen and is said.

Nilanjana Ray in "Resisting Silence and Censorship in Autobiography: Marjane Satrapi" traces the silences that war and trauma induce in women. She taps the form of graphic novels to put together a different narrative of geographical displacement and political upheaval.

Prity Barnwal's paper "Silence as Language of Resistance: A Study of Sontag's Alice in Bed" "attempts to closely dissect Sontag's play Alice in Bed to show how silence is used, represented and practiced in her work". She eschews the derogatory implications of silence and instead sees it more as an alternative means of empowering expression.

Ruchi Nagpal in "Articulating Silence: A Postmodern Appropriation" looks at the idea of 'sublime' as manifested via silence "through 'lack', 'escape', 'unavailability', and 'unrepresentability'". She focuses on certain postmodern instances art which bypass conventional notions of silence.

Shibhashish Purkayastha in "Silence, Shame and Narrative Agency: A Reading of Tito Mukhopadhyay's Beyond the Silence: My Life, the World and Autism" deals with the shame of a disabled life and how in its expression, the narrative form incorporates the self-contradiction or uncertainty inherent in such experiences.

In his concluding remarks, Professor Prasad evoked the metaphor of a 'kitchen' in differentiating between rationality in human beings as "thinking beings" vis-à-vis irrational animals. He commented on the method of processing sensory experiences in the mind and externalising them. Through this, he makes a larger point about political ideologies as a passion or after analysis.

Panel Two: Silence and Resistance

The session was chaired by Dr Vibha Singh Chauhan (Principal, Kirorimal College, University of Delhi.) the session had five presenters presenting on various aspects of silence and its manifestations.

The first paper titled Politics of Silence in Relation to War in Detective Fiction: Understanding the Interrelationship Between War and Gender through Agatha Christie's "*The Mysterious Affair at Styles & N or M?* and Virginia Woolf's *Three Guineas*" was presented by Ratnakar Kumar. The paper talks about 'femininine space' which speaks mostly of silences and a 'masculine space' which is the battlefield or the space of a male detectives in detective fictions.

Swarnika Ahuja's paper titled as "The war emerged in my shrieks: War, Trauma and Narrative Stratergies in Marguetite Duras' Memoir, *The War*" talked about Duras' work provide an anti-war stance from the female author's perspective. The paper further examines the silence deployed as a stratergy to lay bare the incoherence of the war experience.

The third paper titled "Silence in Arundati Roy's novel *The Ministry of Utmost Happiness*" by Anjali Dawar studies the vacuum left by the absence of expressions in the novel which further helps the author to interpret the novel in different ways.

Shantani Das' paper "A Sisterhood of Silenced Voices: Analysing Selected Prison Writing by Women in the Indian Context" analyses the ways in which the ideology of the prosion first re-writes the individual as a criminal through the process of trial and sentencing and then uses mechanism like the marks-system and case file to dictate the terms of prisoner's articulation of own experiences.

The last paper of the session by Sukanta Roy titled "Creating Identity Vis-à-vis Reconstructing History and Engaging with Social Aporias in the Poetry of Rita Dove and Jean Binta Breeze" talks about how the mentioned works analyse mainstream narratives only to deconstruct it and later recreate a new way of perceiving history from personal experience.

Panel Three: Silence and/as Punishment

This session was chaired by Dr. Sucheta Chaturvedi, Associate Professor at Department of English of Lakshmibai College, University of Delhi. The session had a total of three presentations encapsulating various aspects and perspectives regarding silence.

The session began with Aratrika Bose's paper titled, "(Re) Articulation of Alternate Sexuality: Questioning the 'Natural' and the Discursive Limits of Sex" which was a theoretical inquiry into the erasures and exclusions by the 'construction' of the heterosexuality as the 'normative' sexuality; how it resulted in stifling the body's voice, its subjectivity if that voice didn't agree with the nation's heterosexual imperative.

""What more can you do?": Locating the Silent Resilience of the Tortured Body in Mahashweta Devi's Draupadi and Ariel Dorfman's Death and the Maiden" was by Anukriti Jayant in her presentation analyzed how the protagonists of her selected texts had turned their silence, at the moment of extreme torture, into an agency which was much more powerful than the end their perpetrators had tried to achieve.

The last paper by Somya, an viewed The Book of Secrets as a partly commemorative, albeit in a benignly satirical way, of the silenced histories of women during East Africa's encounter with Arab traders, Indian settler communities and European colonialists in her paper, "Gender, the Subaltern and the 'Construction of Silence' in M.G. Vassanji's The Book of Secrets".

The session concluded with Dr Chaturvedi providing her remarks and critical inputs regarding the themes taken up by the presenters vis-à-vis relating with the overall theme, making it an intellectually stimulating and interactive session.

Plenary Session III: (11:00 am – 12:45 pm)

Professor Raj Kumar, Head at Department of English, University of Delhi made the first plenary presentation for the day. Crossing over from the state of subalternity to that of "speaking truth to power" formed the focus of Professor Kumar's paper presentation. He questions the gap between the appearance of the first Indian autobiography in 1641 by a male writer and that of Rasa Sundari, a woman in 1860. Likewise, the publication of the first Dalit autobiography in English in 1951 reflects a silence for Professor

Kumar, as he exposes how the new Dalit discourse and pedagogical practices appear as disturbing for the 'centre'.

Professor H. S. Prasad, Former Head at the Department of Philosophy, University of Delhi followed Professor Kumar with his presentation. In this paper he discusses the conditional nature of human existence, even phenomena such as life and death. He emphasizes sensory experience as the starting point of existence. He finds silence inherent in the suffering of human beings as a community. He makes a case for the "autonomy of an individual through self-effort". In this moving from passion to compassion, he sees a silence operating.

Professor Aruna Broota, Retired Professor at the Department of Psychology, University of Delhi made the concluding Presentation for this panel. In 'Multiple Understandings to the Word Silence', Prof. Broota explores the dangers inherent in singular interpretations of either silence or noise and talk. Vis-à-vis her husband, she feels her "ethnic behaviour" forces her into silence although that does not quell the anger or "noise" within. Through her experience in her clinic, she discusses the significance of "cultural specificities, genetic as well as learnt behaviours" in interpersonal transactions of children. She outlines possible behavioural patterns and reasons behind silence in children.

Panel Discussion (2:00 pm – 3:45 pm)

The concluding session for our Two Day National Conference was moderated by Dr. Sucheta Chaturvedi, Associate Professor at Lakshmibai College, University of Delhi. The panel brought together pioneers from diverse walks of life to deliberate and expand upon the social and cultural dimensions of silence and its pragmatic politics. The panel constituted of eminent film director Mr. Rahul Rawail, former IPS officer Vimla Mehra and two times Rajya Sabha member and managing director of The Pioneer, Dr. Chandan Mitra. With her incisive questions and brilliant comments artfully guiding the flow of the conversation, Dr. Sucheta brought forth the following insights from the members of the panel:

The conversation began with Mr. Rawail providing the audience with perceptive insight into the complicated dynamics between speech and silence, stressing on the differences between noise and sound. Highlighting how silences functions as a universal system of language and its interplay with emotions such as love, pain, desire etc, he reminisces upon his experimentation with the communicative power of silence and sounds; using examples such as his highly popular film Arjun Pandit and the silent opening scene of the same, performance by Om Puri in Akrosh, scenes from the movie Gravity etc. He concluded by reflecting upon the crowding presence of noise in contemporary cinema through the metonymy of Bollywood lyrics, which he viewed as empty loud noise devoid of any and all meaning.

Observations by Mr. Rawail were followed by Smt. Vimla Mehra's mediations on the spiritual and psychic potentialities of silence for the contemporary era. Drawing a necessary distinction between listening and hearing, Smt. Mehra classified the former as an emotional engagement while the latter function simply as an action. Stressing upon the interplay between the human body and silences, she argued how, often body language, personality and tone convey meanings more powerfully than simple acts of speech. Examining silence across a spectrum of positive and negative energies, Smt. Mehra had put forth a definition of silence in her address, which contained within itself reformative possibilities of change and betterment.

Valedictorysession (4:00 pm – 4:45 pm)

The conference was concluded with a riveting valedictory address by Chief Guest Dr. Chandan Mitra. The chair for the session, Dr. Sucheta Chaturvedi welcomed Dr. Mitra with warm words and went on to provide a brief report of the debates, discussions and arguments that were touched upon in the span of the conference. Highlighting how the conference had opened up the myriad interdisciplinary potentialities housed within the gamut of silence and its study, Dr. Chaturvedi then began the session by asking Dr.

Mitra to share his views in silence and its scope with the audience (with special reference to the discipline of History).

Dr. Chandan Mitra began by shedding critical light upon the role and possibilities of silence and its interactions with the disciplines of history and politics. Drawing upon the example of the role of silence in Mahatma Gandhi's radical politics, Dr. Mitra cited the successful role of 'mon vrat' or self imposed vow of silence in Gandhi's struggle against British colonial powers. He made the case for reading into the gaps and fissures of History and the power of silencing that accompanies it; for arriving at an alternative narrative wherein the previously invisible subaltern starts to emerge. Exploring the discursive possibilities of silence and its engagement with violence as its counter, Dr. Mitra further gave the examples of Nelson Mandela, Gandhi and others to put forth a case, for the subversive use of silence against violence as a crucial tool for politics and protests in the twenty first century.

The session came to a close with Dr. Mitra address, after which the floor was then opened up for questions and discussion. The audience presented Dr. Mitra with questions regarding his engagement with silence in the field of history and journalism. He responded to each question in detail and with perceptive insights. Following this, Dr. Mitra and Principal Pratyush Vatsala felicitated all the paper presenters with certificates.

Vote of Thanks: Convener, Pratyush Vatsala Tripathi

The valedictory session marked the conclusion of the two day conference on silence which had opened multiple pathways into an intense and diverse investigation into the multifaceted nature of silence across a plethora of academic disciplines. The same was highlighted in the closing speech delivered by our esteemed principal who provided a fitting closure to the conference. Extending her gratitude to the various esteemed panelists and speakers who made the seminar a truly enriching experience for one and all present, Dr. Vatsala gratefully recognized the contributions made by each and every speaker to the discourse on silence and its many tangents. Furthermore, acknowledging the many hours of tireless work and efforts put into making this conference a success, she extended her heartfelt gratitude to the faculty members of the Department of English (with special regards to the organizing committee) and the wide network of non teaching technical and administrative staff without whom the conference could not have turned out to be the success that it achieved. She also extended her praise to the hard work of student volunteers of the English Department. She closed her speech by asking all present to carry forth the ideas and debates born out the two days of scintillating and rigorous academic engagement into our daily lives, by reading and exploring the myriad possibilities and meanings of silence and the effervescent power it yields over all our lives.

Technical Committee
Brijesh, Minakshi,
Shruti, Aanchal

List of Contributors

ANJALI VERMA - M.Phil. Psychoanalytic Psychotherapy, (School of Human Studies), Ambedkar University Delhi.

SHIBANI PHUKAN - Assistant Professor, Atma Ram Sanatan Dharm CollegeUniversity of Delhi, New Delhi.

GAURAV KUMAR - Junior Research Fellow, UGCM. Phil Scholar at Department of Comparative Literature and Translation Studies, Ambedkar University, Delhi.

PRAJAKTA SIMON - Research Scholar (Ph.D), Centre for English Studies, School of Language, Literature and Culture Studies, Jawaharlal Nehru University, New Delhi-67.

MERCY JILL JILL - PhD Researcher, Department of Comparative LiteratureUniversity of Delhi.

JYOTI SINGH - Research Scholar (PhD), Department of English, University of Delhi.

PROF (DR.) SUBRAMANIAN RAMAN IYER - Provost Vice Chancellor, Shri. Venkateshwara University.

MS. HIMANI SHARMA - Research Scholar, IGDTUW, Kahmere Gate.

Dr. SHWETA SENGAR - Assistant Professor, Lakshmibai College, University of Delhi.

PRIYA V - Fellow, SAHAPEDIA-UNESCO, BANGALORE.

REHA KEER - PhD Research Scholar, USHSS, GGSIP University.

SANGEETA JAWLA - PhD English, Ambedkar University Delhi, Lothian Road, Kashmere Gate, Pin-110006, Old Delhi.

SANTU NEOG - Assistant Professor, Department of English, Shyama Prasad Mukherji College (for Women).

SWASTI SHARMA - Assistant Professor, Department of English, Satyawati College, University of Delhi, Delhi.

GAGANDEEP KAUR AHLUWALIA - School of Human Studies, Ambedkar University Delhi.

NILANJANA RAY - MPhil Scholar, Department of English, University of Delhi.

RUCHI NAGPAL - M.Phil/Ph.D., Department of English, Jamia Millia Islamia.

SHIBASHISH PURKAYASTHA - Ph.D Research Scholar (English), Department of Humanities and Social Sciences, IIT, Guwahati.

SWARNIKA AHUJA - Research Scholar, Department of English, University of Delhi.

SUKANTA ROY - Research Scholar, Department of English, University of Delhi.

ARATRIKA BOSE - Research Scholar, Department of Languages, Christ (Deemed) University.